# Anti-Booze Crusaders in Victorian Liverpool

Tim Malcolm

First Published 2005 by Countyvise Limited,
14 Appin Road, Birkenhead, Wirral CH41 9HH.



The author has made every reasonable effort to contact all copyright holders. Any errors/omissions that may have occurred are inadvertent and regretted, and anyone who, for any reason, has not been contacted is invited to write to the publishers so that full acknowledgement may be made in subsequent editions of this work.

British Library Cataloguing in Publication Data.
A catalogue record for this book is available from the British Library.

Please note: From 1st January 2007 ISBNs will contain 13 numbers these numbers will be the same as the present number printed below the barcode (ie. starting 978).
Countyvise is showing both existing (10 digit) and future (13 digit) ISBNs on the Title page verso. Please continue to use the 10 figure number until 31st December 2006.

ISBN 1 901231 63 1 ISBN 978 1 901231 63 2

# Contents

# Introduction

Temperance may seem a rather dry subject and indeed much of the literature on the subject is certainly that. Textbooks and tracts contain vast deserts of arid prose, but there is the occasional oasis. The authors of these oases were often dramatic, flamboyant and self-opinionated writers. Selection of individuals for the present work is not meant to be representative, rather they have been chosen on account of their prejudiced and colourful views, sometimes expressed in biographies and autobiographies. Their conscientious and much-needed work to combat the evils of drink is readily acknowledged and the accounts that follow are in no way meant to diminish their sterling efforts, but are merely to illustrate the mixture of motives and prejudices present at the time.

Class, religion, politics (at a local and national level), together with American influences are intertwined in temperance work in Liverpool. Immigration, especially from Ireland, but also from Scotland and Wales in the case of temperance workers, is also important. Those who wrote temperance history-books at the time admitted there were thousands of names that were, sadly, forgotten. It may be noted that most of the names are male, women tended not to blow their own trumpet and few blew it for them. Further they were engaged in practical work with those in need. Margaret Simey in her detailed study of Liverpool in the 19th century, does devote an entire chapter to *Women in charitable work: feminine philanthropy 1852-1870.*

Excessive drinking was an all-pervading problem in Victorian Liverpool. The second city of the Empire was second to none in its promulgation of the vices and the virtues of the period. Among the former were drunkenness and its consequences and among the latter the efforts of religious and philanthropic workers, who fought against alcohol abuse and its evil social effects.

Cold statistics such as death rates directly due to drink, or high infant mortality rates at least partly due to its effects, can be read in the reports of statutory bodies. Descriptive accounts appear in the evidence given to Select Committees, which were set up to address the problem. From these, much hand wringing ensued but little practical help. This had to be organised by the various churches and humanitarian organisations.

The temperance movement originally campaigned for just that, the temperate use of alcohol. However from the mid 1830s total abstinence, rather than just moderation, was considered to be the only way of breaking the vicious circle of drunkenness, poverty, squalor and morbidity often ending in death. How did temperance workers go about the business of persuading the populace to give up drink? How did "The Trade", the producers and purveyors, of alcohol react? How did politics at a local and national level react to these, potentially fundamental, changes to Britain's social system?

**Victorian**

Queen Victoria reigned from 1837 to 1901, but the Victorian period is often taken to include the years to 1910, the reign of her son Edward VII. For much of the 20th century the term "Victorian" was one of disapproval. At best it could imply an old fashioned attitude, at worst, inflexible authoritarianism.

However, a more enlightened attitude is now evident and the valuable contributions to our society from that period are now being recognised. Lytton Strachey in his *Eminent Victorians* (1918) was a satirical biographer of four, until then, eminent citizens. This book may be compared to Tristram Hunt's well received *New Jerusalem* (2004) in which he praises the work done by Victorian leaders of urban society. He describes the building of great cities and their institutions through the lives of their Victorian champions. He singles out Liverpool's William Roscoe (son of a Mount Pleasant publican) describing him as "a cultural lynchpin in the development of the Victorian city".

In recent years there have been many successful television programmes on Victorian pioneers, inventors, industrialists etc. Fred Dibnah marvelled at their machines, Adam Hart-Davies evocatively titles his contribution *What the Victorians did for us*, largely beneficial in his view. A popular series was *Restoration*, won by Manchester's Victoria Baths, (actually Edwardian). Well known television personalities search for their roots, their family history, which is often found in Victorian times. Nationally, "Victorian" has been rehabilitated.

In Liverpool, the city of culture 2008, the Victorian building heritage is now much appreciated. "The flavour of the city is Victorian and Edwardian" (Quentin Hughes). St George's Hall (1841-56) is pristine again, as is the North Western Station hotel (1871) and Lime Street station (1867). Joseph Sharples' excellent book *Liverpool* describes the city's magnificent Victorian heritage. Nowadays the need for conservation is more recognised than when Ted Hubbard, the Victorian Society and others had to campaign to save the Albert Dock complex from destruction (1971). Robert Cain, the brewer, enhanced Liverpool's townscape with his glorious pubs, the Philharmonic Hotel (1898), The Vines (1907) and the Crown (1905). These are now established on the tourist trail, possibly to the chagrin of Victorian temperance worthies. The Philharmonic has been described in a recent English Heritage publication as "England's most magnificent public house" (Brandwood et al.). Freddie O'Connor treats us to a comprehensive tour of the old public houses of Liverpool in his four volume set *A Pub on Every Corner* and there are a lot of corners.

Temperance Halls have now all gone, or been converted to other uses. Terry Cavanagh, in his 370 pages on Liverpool's public sculptures, can only list two Temperance monuments. In the first a female figure, pouring water from a pitcher, represents "temperance". This statue was part of a drinking fountain erected to commemorate Hannah Mary Thom (nee Rathbone) and her charitable work for the poor. She was the wife of the Rev. J. H. Thom. A similar representation of temperance is described on a relief in St George's Hall, with the motto "add to knowledge temperance". Here Temperance is diluting Baccus' wine (A. J. Richardson).

There were many dark sides to Victorian life. Pubs may have been the only place to obtain warmth, shelter and company, but the obligatory drinking extracted a terrible price. Appalling hardship ensued. Many people and organisations tried to combat this evil or at least mitigate the sad effects on individuals and families in Liverpool.

**Drink in Victorian Literature**

*Her Benny*, written by Silas K. Hocking (1850-1935) a Methodist minister in Liverpool, is a well-known account of social deprivation caused by poverty and drink. Hocking had first-hand knowledge of the effects drunkenness had on children and family life. A less melodramatic account, more factual, is given by H Shimmin who wrote a series of descriptive articles in the *Porcupine*. Several of his contributions have been reprinted and discussed by Walton and Wilcox. Little seemed to have changed by the end of the century, Pat O'Mara describes his childhood and the similar social violence induced by drink. It must not be thought that these problems were peculiar to Liverpool. The Dundee poet William McGonagall wrote several poems on the subject. The most famous *The Demon Drink* is well worth reading in full, it opens:

*Oh thou demon drink, thou fell destroyer,*
*thou curse of society, and its greatest annoyer,*
*What hast thou done to society, let me think?*
*I answer thou hast caused most of ills, thou demon drink.*

He continues to list the many and various problems in his own famous doggerel. This poem, together with his *Little Match Girl*, may be read as a prècis of *Her Benny*.

Drink, if not the only reason for such sadness, was seen as the main cause. However another cause may have been the indifference shown by the middle and upper classes to this violence and suffering. They themselves were far from sober but their behaviour was hidden, it was certainly not written about.

In the absence of television and popular press, one way of influencing working-class attitudes was via poetry and songs which could be used at religious or temperance gatherings. John Kirton, author of several temperance books, published 250 pages of verses "suitable for social meetings". These verses focused on children and their parents and the evils of drink. He warned each family member in turn of the dangers.

The pub
*It is lighted we know like a palace, that fair-gilded temple of sin,*
*It has signs on the walls let us read them, rum wine whisky brandy and gin.*
*Beware though you think you may need them, my son Oh my son, don't go in.*

Young boy
*Drunk in the streets Oh saddest sight, a boy of fourteen years*
*Some mothers darling fallen low, in vain her falling tears.*
*A father's hopes were fondly raised, that his young son might grow*
*To be a bright and shining light and every virtue know.*

Fallen mother
*Oh mother dear mother don't leave us again, alone as you did yesterday,*
*We were lonely and cold for the fire went out, and we 'most too hungry to play.*

Fallen father
*For father at the alehouse stays, whilst mother weeps alone*
*And little Charlie even cries, for bread and there is none.*

There are common themes running through most offerings. The children are starving and destitute, usually alone in an icy garret, except when running shoeless through the streets selling matches or in searching for their parents, often in well-lit drinking dens. Though children beseech their parents to reform, death, for young and old alike, is the usual outcome. These songs do not make for jovial social get-togethers, but in Victorian times such themes were accepted, life was harder and death more frequent. Legislative remedies are considered in some songs but with more hope than expectation.

*Ye senators of England, ye Christian men and true*
*Ten hundred thousand children, in anguish call to you.*
*Their eyes are red with weeping, their forms are bruised and bare*
*Their hearts with joy once leaping, are racked with pain and care.*

Who were these senators and what was their response? Some of the more interesting personalities and their activities are described in the following pages.

**Relevance of temperance today**

In the 1800s the temperance movement spent much time and energy in trying to persuade the individual to be temperate or even abstinent and the government to legislate to stop, or at least to curb, the sale of alcohol in public houses. Today a similar debate is on-going concerning smoking in public houses. It is interesting that New York, Ireland, Scotland and Liverpool lead the way in today's anti-smoking crusade as visitors from these places played a large part in developing temperance on Merseyside. *The Times* (October 28th 2005 p16) reports,"Pubs in the most deprived areas are most likely to choose smoking over food", if there has to be a choice.

To ignore history is to be condemned to re-live it. Liverpool during the1860s, in an effort to reduce the adverse effects of drinking, expanded the opportunity to buy alcohol by greatly increasing available outlets. This action was well intentioned, but it was a naive hope that flooding the market would lead to reduction. In retrospect the outcome was obvious, increased consumption. Today in an effort to reduce drunkenness, potential 24-hour drinking in public houses is proposed. (See **End piece**).

In Sweden, a referendum to join the euro was influenced to a great extent by the 300,000 temperance members in that country who were opposed to the drinking laws of the E.C. (Daily Telegraph, Sept.15th 2003, p. 4). In this book frequent references are made to current debates, with quotations from recent newspaper articles.

# Taking the pledge

## The Pledge

Success, in temperance circles, often simply meant the numbers of people taking the pledge. The word "taking" seems to be used in two senses. Firstly, the individual could "take" the pledge, make a personal promise to avoid alcohol. The second sense would be the number of pledges taken by the temperance speaker at a meeting. He, and it was usually a male, could claim to have taken a hundred pledges that night, or several thousands over a weekend! There were various types of pledges in use. These could be

*for a limited time, e.g. one year*
*until a certain age was reached, e.g. 18 or 21*
*to avoid only strong spirits, beer being acceptable*
*to include all visitors to one's house*
*to include all one's employees*
*allowing communion wine (considerable controversy)*
*allowing alcohol prescribed by a doctor (a common practice)*
*"cordials" were usually allowed but often contained alcohol*

## Results

What was the effect of taking the pledge and how was any success estimated? Simple numbers of people taking the pledge were regularly reported in the literature of the time but these numbers are, at the least, unconvincing. The figures given are very rounded, apart from being very large. It may be wondered if many people took, and retook, the pledge at every meeting they attended. To be seen not taking it might be seen as implying an intention to continue drinking. The individual's desire to conform in a crowd is often overwhelming. Other measures of beneficially influencing drinking behaviour are sometimes advanced e.g. reductions in

*numbers of pubs, or income of publicans*
*tax revenue*
*numbers in police cells*
*numbers brought before the magistrates*
*numbers convicted of drunken assaults etc.*

It would be hard, especially in the Victorian age, to measure improvement in social functioning of the individual, and his family. This would be a true measure of success. Industrialists might see improvement in attendance at work and less accidents, leading to increased production, as a desirable outcome.

Widespread overt and covert opposition to pledge taking came from many vested interests who wanted to preserve the status quo. These included publicans, brewers, distillers, and the landlords of cellar dwellings in Liverpool whose accommodation might be rejected by a more sober, possibly more affluent, workforce. The landed gentry might fear a fall in demand for their barley with consequent impoverishment of rural workers. Nationally the Exchequer stood to lose very considerably. There were many opponents.

# Ministers of Religion

The inherent immorality of drunkenness and its most adverse effects on individuals, families and society led religious bodies to act against it. Activity included practical help in the home, education, provision of entertainment and advocacy of temperance or abstinence. In Liverpool there are many famous ministers associated with these efforts, some will later be considered .

**Catholics**

Advice for Catholics, especially the young, was detailed in *The Catholic Temperance Reader* by Rev. W. H. Cologan (Hon. Sec. Catholic Truth Society) and Sir F. R. Cruise (past President Royal College of Physicians, Ireland). This book contained 20 chapters on the effects of alcohol and drunkenness on the individual. There are many direct quotes from Roman Catholic bishops. "Drunkenness is a sin of the flesh .... notorious amongst Catholics..... children of drunken fathers and mothers are born with the taint .... sickened and weakened" (Cardinal Vaughan). " Drink is dragging thousands of Irish men and Irish women down into hell" (Cardinal McCabe). "For all Christians, the law of temperance is an obligation" (Bishop of Shrewsbury). Such sentiments were endorsed by Pope Leo XIII.

Cardinal Manning condemned parents who sent their children to public houses to fetch beer and spirits, A practice prohibited in Liverpool only in 1909. He took a wider view, drink "Paralysed productiveness of our industries and destroyed the indigenous races wheresoever the British Empire is in contact with them".

The *Reader* reported that in 1891, the Catholics of the United Kingdom, which was taken to include Ireland, spent £26,000,000 on drink, assuming that Catholics spent as much on drink as the rest of the population! It was calculated that for the price of a pint a day for a year, Catholics could pay to construct Westminster Cathedral - it must be admitted that some of the figures and calculations are a little difficult to follow!

Thomas Burke published the *Catholic History of Liverpool* in 1910. The social and drink problems of the 19th century are vividly described.

Father Noble, and his temperance organisation at Bispham Street saw drink as the " Deadly enemy to Catholic progress ".

**Father James Nugent**

Fr. Nugent was probably the first Catholic priest to be ordained in Liverpool (1846) and was called the second Father Mathew. He was said to have regarded the temperance crusade as the greatest work of his life and he had had many great works. Nugent founded the (temperance) "League of the Cross". Branches of this league grew to have 30,000 members. The work was personally endorsed by Archbishop Manning (1874), though his involvement was embroiled in local politics.

Cannon Bennett, in his biography of Father Nugent, describes the first object that Irish immigrants saw on arrival in Liverpool, St Patrick with Shamrock in hand, on the wall of an Irish public house. Not quite the Statue of Liberty. Great similarities between Father Mathew and Father Nugent are discussed. Bennett records that Nugent "delivered some home truths about the publicans in Scotland Road being the only dealers doing any trade.....he was intolerant and contemptuous towards those who were doing time (in prison) on account of their insobriety". Nugent was the official Catholic chaplain to the Borough gaol from 1863. Cardinal Manning repeatedly tried to persuade Nugent to come to London to run the League of the Cross there, but it was Nugent who brought Manning to Liverpool to speak on several occasions.

**The Irish Pub**

The public house played a most important role in Liverpool Irish society and not just for drinking. Prof. John Belchem, Liverpool University, has described its various facets. For many, without a permanent address, it was a sort of poste-restante where letters, and much else, could be collected. For those arriving from rural Ireland it was a haven in a frightening metropolis. Some new arrivals may not have had English, only Irish Gaelic. For all it was a rendezvous to meet one's compatriots. Ireland was then part of the United Kingdom, so though there were consulates and delegations from many countries of the world in this great seaport, there was no Irish consulate. Perhaps the Irish pub took that role.

Margaret Simey, in her classic *Charitable Effort in Liverpool in the 19th Century* writes that "to people newly uprooted from rural life the mere size of Liverpool must have been daunting and identification with some familiar group such as that of church or chapel a matter of necessity". The Irish Pub could also fill that role.

A modern version of the "Irish pub" has spread over the world, even two in Kemerovo (Central Russia), *The Barge* and *The Pint.* Grand Cayman has the *Fidel Murphy*! They are relatively uncommon in Ireland where pubs are now clean and smoke-free. Some "Irish pubs" have been prepared for English rowdies in the Temple Bar area of Dublin.

**Rev. J. Jones**

Rev. John Jones repeatedly called attention to the dire social consequence of excessive drinking e.g. in his *The Slain in Liverpool in 1866 by Drink.* He believed that the "angel of mercy" (philanthropy) should visit each "lazar-house" (houses of drunks). "We wish to invest the miserable drunkard with the value which is stamped upon every other human and immortal being, and thus to rescue him from the neglect and contempt of those who pass him by as unworthy of their notice".

Jones goes on to describe drinking habits in Liverpool "Barrels and bottles have been the most popular commodity in this commercial emporium. Drink, strong drink, seems the ever growing order of the day. Social hospitality is felt to be robbed of half its meaning unless it be dealt out in the shape of alcoholic beverage". The ensuing numbers of deaths due to drink, he critically evaluates. True numbers are, in his view, far higher than official records allow. The victims are predominantly lower class, as determined by their occupation, and Irish, as determined by their names. Jones believes that it is the situation amongst the Irish already in Liverpool, that corrupts new Irish immigrants. His last sentence is, "If we do not try, what will He say who is the judge of all the earth, and who has appointed every man to be his brother's keeper?".

**Rev. R H Lundie**

The Rev. Robert Henry Lundie (Presbyterian) in his pamphlet *The Dark Side of Liverpool* (1880) does indeed give a dark and depressing picture of Liverpool life. He despairs of his people's lives and of his inability to improve them. He describes the squalor and gnawing poverty, the poor clothing and furniture in their homes. He sees the thriving public house and pawnbroker "Like a fungus sucking the living sap out of the district". He realises that if children have no respect for their drunken parents, they will develop no respect for authority. He admits these people have little or no recognisable connection with church or chapel and acknowledges that his visits have "No more mark than a swallow's wing" in improving conditions. He admits that he may be rescuing only one in 500, rescuing children to go to a purer home in Canada. He despairs that on the "desolate region locally we have not wrought the slightest change, it remains dirty, drunken, dissolute and diseased". He is appalled that in the city centre there are 46 public houses within 150 yards of the Sailors' Home. He hopes the new suburbs will be free of the gangrene. (see Geographical Prohibition).

**Rev. R C Armstrong**

Ten years later, the Rev. Armstrong wrote in similar terms in the *Deadly Shame of Liverpool, an appeal to the Municipal Voters*. In this account he again describes squalor and dissolute behaviour, but he also denounces the indifference of the middle and upper classes. He writes that after he had been six years in the "second city of the mightiest empire the world has ever seen", he is concerned that he too may become indifferent to the suffering and accept the great divide between "The gay equipages rolling down Bold Street, with the brilliant shop fronts, and the gaunt faces of the poor and abandoned".

A. N. Wilson in *The Victorians* also describes the divide between rich and poor. In London "the poor simply were not allowed into Piccadilly. Even quite bourgeois streets and squares were gated and barred against proletarian ingress".

Armstrong notes the "indifferent air of so many who might have been helpers...custom deadens all emotions". He believes that "an evil as horrible and as subtle and complex as American slavery itself is at our door here in Liverpool. The evil, is the knitting together of the wholesale liquor trade, of drunkenness and of prostitution on an enormous scale in one vast compact interest, and the power that interest has obtained within the governing bodies of Liverpool". Armstrong believes prostitution to be an essential part of public house life which "sets the gold flowing towards the coffers of the great brewers". He claimed that Lime Street, Church Street and Parker Street were the rendezvous for young men and courtesans. He complained that one public house was fined £5 for having "seventy-five loose women" but its licence was not endorsed. Though pubs closed at 11 p.m cabs then took their customers to houses ready to receive them. He believed the police knew of 443 brothels, but their response was less effective than in other northern towns. In Manchester one publican was convicted per 51 drunkards convicted, in Liverpool the ratio was one per 2873.

His, more optimistic, 1892 report tells us that the new chairman of the watch committee Mr Henry H. Hornby is respected. The previous chairman, Alderman John Hughes who also sat on the licensing bench, had been the "confidential legal adviser of the two largest public house owners in Liverpool". In Armstrong's opinion "Conservatism in Liverpool is inextricably bound up with the brewing interest. Visit the Toxteths on an election day and count how many of Mr Robert Caine's drays are plying the streets to carry voters to the poll".

**Rev. Abraham Hume**

Rev. Hume was the incumbent of the new parish of Vauxhall when he wrote in strong terms of Liverpool's vices. He saw the very clear distinction between the rich and the poor. He condemned "immorality" which he divided into two; "intemperance" and "the social evil", the latter was to be attacked by the "Society for Suppression of Vicious Practices" which would "purify our streets". He supported the confining of such activities to specific areas "fever better confined to hospital than diffused among the entire population". This is currently proposed, "Liverpool Councillors voted overwhelmingly.....to open a managed site

....away from residential streets ....sex workers to entertain clients inside a compound surveyed by CCTV .... between 8pm and 2am each day". (Times newspaper, 27th Jan. 2005).

Hume's pamphlet contains a most interesting map *Liverpool Ecclesiastical and Social* which he produced for the National Association for the Promotion of Social Science in October 1858. He clearly indicates "pauper streets, semi-pauper streets, streets of crime and immorality, etc". He further indicates the areas where cholera and violent deaths are prevalent and discusses the overprovision of public houses.

**Revivalist Preachers**

Many temperance crusaders were ministers of religion. Their methods of persuasion make interesting reading. In Victorian times, a powerful preacher could have the most dramatic effect on his congregation or audience. Today people are less susceptible, more sophisticated, critical even cynical. In the 19th century there were no TV's, radios or cinemas. A charismatic speaker could deeply influence his listeners, especially if they were members of a large crowd.

The ways of manipulating audiences and the resulting amazing behaviour, sometimes termed mass-hysteria, have been discussed by William Sargant, a psychiatrist who held controversial views (1957). He describes how politicians and religious leaders can harangue and then dominate the minds of their listeners resulting in conversion, e.g. to temperance. Repeated chanting or singing, often over long periods, can lead to states of exhaustion and increased suggestibility, that is the suspension of an individual's critical judgement. The crowd acts as one with a single mind, as if hypnotised. In this state, the Mesmer-like leader can impose his beliefs on his audience. Sargant quotes Salmon (1859), a traditional religious leader who, though critical of his evangelistic Revivalist colleagues, has to admit " no room to doubt that the Revival movement .....has been attended by the suppression of drunkenness". It would seem that the newly acquired behaviour of individuals can last at least for some time.

**Rev. R Aitken**

Is such activity relevant in Liverpool? Picton (1873) describes the effect produced by the preaching of Rev. Robert Aitken, whose over enthusiastic methods had caused his separation from the Church of England and from the Wesleyan Methodists. Picton in his classic *Memorials of Liverpool* writes "The excitement created became difficult to control (so) in about 1837 the Chapel in Hope Street was erected by his friends and for a time a large amount of excitement was kept up by his energetic ministrations". The Rev Dr. Thom's description of a service follows. "The place was crowded almost to suffocation, his language was pointed and energetic, his manner impassioned, occasionally indeed bordering on the wildest enthusiasm …. reaching his conclusion or climax many of the audience (were) apparently unable to control themselves. When the preacher had ended, an invitation to go downstairs was given to such as felt inclined to do so. …. In the apartment below ….. persons some grovelling on their bellies some joyful, but all more or less excited and the majority uttering a great variety of exclamations". This behaviour is typical of that described by Sargant as taking place in many and various places across the globe. Picton concludes that Mr (sic) Aitken abruptly left town. The present author recalls not dissimilar, far from religious, behaviour in these lower rooms in the 1960s. The Everyman Theatre is now there.

**Rev. C. F. Aked**

In 1897, Rev. T. W. M. Lund preached a sermon in Liverpool, later published in the press, in which he attacked the temperance movement and teetotallers for being "New Ascetics". Rev. Aked saw this as being most insulting, so he too preached a sermon, at the Pembroke Chapel Liverpool, which was then published as a temperance tract. He wrote "an ascetic is one who denies himself a pleasure, because he believes that pleasure is sinful. A teetotaller is one who abstains from alcohol because he believes it to be a deadly poison". He points out that health, and indeed happiness, ensue in the absence of alcohol.

He considers the rights of the non-drinking individual in society, "Drinking is an interference with the liberty of the non-drinker…. drinking encroaches upon the non-drinker's right to security in a community of which he is a member". It is significant that he entitled his sermon "England Free and Sober". In 2005 we are still discussing this balance; the right of an individual to drink to excess but with consequent adverse effects on the rights of other people.

**American Preachers**

Many temperance meetings were far removed from those described above. Some people may have found meetings repetitive, even dull, speaker after speaker on the negative aspects of drink. These were well known and, presumably, agreed by most in the audience. Light relief could be provided by Temperance bands with hymns and songs. But to combat boredom and to present a fresh view on the same theme, visiting speakers were popular. Perhaps temperance leaders' credibility was enhanced by such endorsements, any self-doubts were quashed.

American preachers were always popular, especially in Liverpool with its strong shipping connections to The States. Picton describes the visit of Messrs Dwight Lyman Moody and Ira David Sankey from the United States in 1875 and 1883. In advance of their visits a committee had erected a hall to hold 10,000 people, the expense of £5000 "was readily subscribed". Picton mentions the "sensational advertising and business management", even in 1875, which had preceded the visit. This had resulted in "the public mind being wound up to the highest pitch of expectation". Such a mind-set is ripe for successful indoctrination. The hall and nearby buildings were filled to overflowing for three services a day for a month. "Catchy tunes were sung by the assembled thousand.... a thrill of mesmeric influence ran through the assembled multitudes...". With an audience prepared in this way, with heightened suggestibility, almost anything is possible, even vows to give up drink.

The *Porcupine*, in1875, devoted much space to a critical appraisal of Moody & Sankey's activities. Their mission was "the latest and greatest sensation in religious revivalism". At their packed meetings "the religious atmosphere (was) infected by the enthusiasm of the two men". Mr Moody was "rough and ready", Mr Sankey had "grace" and was "attractive" in manner. (Feb.13th p.728-9). The *Porcupine* questioned the "permanence" of their influence. The following week Feb. 20th (p.740-1) there was even more direct criticism. "The sensationalism of the Moody and Sankey meetings deepens as they proceed, and the vulgar strength of expression, noticeable and excusable in the first appeals, has increased till the point of irreverence and blasphemy has been passed". Even the *Porcupine* "dare not repeat" what was said, but the "tone and suggestivness ....are abhorrent to every reverent mind". Feb.27th (p.756-7) , chides "the clergymen of Liverpool who are continually dancing round the coat-tails of Messrs. Sankey and Moody......flunkies of these gentlemen". On March 6th (p.780-1) and March 13th (p.790-1) there is considerable correspondence in support of the American preachers.

J. R. Kaighin in his history of *Bygone Birkenhead* recalls another American, John B. Gough, who achieved "prodigious results, his dramatic oratory and flaming passion captured the listener and bore him away. He could sound the deeps of human nature and fuse the soul". He did all this in the unlikely setting of the Theatre Royal, Argyle Street, Birkenhead and in Hegler's Circus, Liverpool. Kaighin also mentions a " Hibernian called Phillips who would use his ready wit and persuasiveness" to get his listeners to sign the pledge. He had his regular pitch in the open air behind the police offices in Birkenhead.

In more recent times the Evangelist Billy Graham was able to fill Anfield, and the pitch, with huge crowds to hear his powerful preaching. Father Patrick Peyton was another visiting American Evangelist who attracted great numbers to his crusade.

**John Finch**

Though Liverpool imported Father Theobald Mathew the city had already exported John Finch, "The king of the teetotallers" to Ireland in the 1830s for four visits. The life of Finch, a Liverpool iron-merchant has been detailed by R. B. Rose who describes him as a visionary socialist, a man ahead of his time, a disciple and associate of Robert Owen and a powerful temperance reformer. As a Unitarian and philanthropist he strove to improve the lives of the lower classes in Liverpool. He supported practical self-help, founding a Co-operative society in 1829, thirty years before the Rochdale version reached Liverpool.

He opposed the established system of casual labour on the docks by which men were paid in particular public houses at the end of the week. Not to support that pub reduced the chances of further employment. To combat this system he founded the Liverpool Dock Labourers' Society in 1831 investing considerable time and money in what should, in theory, have been a successful enterprise. Vested interests, cheap "Celtic labour" and drunkenness destroyed the organisation.

His direct approach to problems could involve his dealing with individuals, as well as groups. On one occasion he went to Preston to pursue his firm's unpaid debt of £110 and found chronic insobriety of the proprietor to be the problem. He persuaded his customer to take the pledge, so successfully that Thomas Swindlehurst became nationally known as "The king of the reformed drunkards". Finch saw drunkenness as an ever present evil which destroyed the lives of working-class families - as usual upper-class drinking was not mentioned. He was a founder member in 1830 of the Liverpool Temperance Society. By 1834 he had moved from advocating temperance to teetotalism, so persuaded by his now business partner, Swindlehurst.

By 1833 his more intrusive and radical socialist tendencies were apparent. His letter to the *Mercury*, 4th January, proposed the removal of children from houses which were full of vice, misery and drunkenness, for their instruction in more virtuous habits. He advocated boarding schools for infants to the age of nine and training colleges thereafter. This potential disruption of family life met with much opposition. More reasonably he advocated replacement of slum dwellings by municipal housing programmes. His work as an iron merchant enabled him to travel the country. His years of preaching and teaching made him a convincing lecturer. With this combination he obtained 20,000 pledges during visits all over the country, foreshadowing Father Mathew. Finch visited Ireland each year from 1833 to 1836. There he found the living conditions of the lower classes to be even worse than those in Liverpool. Drunkenness was largely to blame. In 1836 in Dublin and Belfast he took over 1600 pledges and formed 30 new societies. It would be interesting to know of any meeting with Mathew.

Finch's views were sought and recorded by the Select Committee inquiring into working-class drunkenness (1834). Finch blamed the wealthy and powerful for not providing alternative amusements. On Sundays parks were closed, pubs were open. He proposed the opening of community centres. Rose describes Finch's further activities in opening the Liverpool Hall of Science in Lord Nelson Street (1840), coffee houses, reading rooms etc. Mrs Rathbone had morally and financially supported Finch and Owen in their plans for social reform, offering £1000 towards Owenite communities.

Finch's life work was to improve the lives of working-class people. Drunkenness was one, perhaps the most important of several factors. As time went on and he became more battle-hardened he advocated sobriety in a setting of socialism, not in a setting of religion. He attempted to interpret the Scriptures to fit his model. This led to tensions within the temperance movement, which retained close contact with established religion. His writings on these matters led to his expulsion in 1837 from the Liverpool Total Abstinence Society. He felt that the mainstream temperance movement saw the working-class as inherently degenerate, rejoicing in drink, so in need of correction. Drunkenness was their original sin. As Rose writes, " The sad decay and final collapse of the Dock Labourers' Society were seized on, not without a kind of triumph, by temperance propagandists as evidence of the fundamental innate sinfulness of the working class".

## Theobald Mathew "The Apostle of Temperance"

**Liverpool 1843 1849 1854**.

In 1843 the parishioners of St Peter's, Seel Street invited Father Theobald Mathew to come to Liverpool and lead an attack on drunkenness in the city, 6000 people signed the petition to invite him (Burke's *Catholic History of Liverpool*).

Mathew was a Catholic monk, working with poorest of the poor in Cork, in Ireland. How was he to become a regular house guest of one of Liverpool's leading families, the Rathbones, have his convalescence in Madeira paid for by Lord Sefton, be lauded in the House of Lords, lionised by Congress in America, and given a personal pension of £ 300 a year by Queen Victoria? There may be two simple reasons. He had, in today's language, charisma and he was selling a most desirable product, Sobriety.

To appreciate this, apparently surprising, transition from one social world to another, we need to know a little of his background. Two of his biographers, Maguire and Kerrigan, provide most interesting details. He was born in 1790 "in a noble mansion in a still nobler demesne", the house of his uncle, Baron Llandaff, in Tipperary. The castle had forty guest-rooms and was far from a "dry" establishment. Not all the family were Catholic, but a costly suit of vestments and a valuable chalice were ready for "the priest in the family". Theobald had eight brothers. He had attended a good school and later Maynooth College, but then joined the Capuchin Order, "the lowest and least influential" friars in Ireland. He worked with the poor and destitute. As a Governor in Cork workhouse during the 1832 cholera epidemic he met many "dilapidated drunkards", so when in 1838 he was approached by William Martin, a Quaker, and the Rev .N. Dunscombe, a Protestant, he joined their temperance crusade, but only after considerable reflection.

He had previously believed moderate drinking "enhanced the delights of friendly intercourse". He acknowledged the "habits, customs.... of the Irish people". He recognised that many were dependent on the manufacture and sale of alcoholic beverages, especially in Cork. Some in his own family were later "totally and absolutely ruined" by his success. His brother had been one of the largest distillers in Ireland. Further, much of his earlier charitable work had been supported by "The Trade". Once embarked on his crusade against Drink his progress was rapid, 1,800,000 had signed the pledge by 1840 and by 1843 six million of his countrymen had done so! (Winskill, vol ii p. 185).

In the summer of 1843 Mathew landed in Liverpool for the first of three visits. His success as the Apostle of Temperance was well known in Ireland, but what would be his acceptance by the English establishment? Earlier that year a public meeting had been called in Dublin, to honour him. He had been feted by two Dukes, four Marquises, nineteen Earl's, ten viscounts, forty baronets, thirty MPs etc, quite a calling-card to bring to England. He attended the ninth annual festival of the Liverpool Total Abstinence Societies, taking nearly 50,000 pledges that weekend 15th -16th July and a further 8,000 at St Anthony's, Scotland Road.

Mathew worked and preached at several other places in Liverpool, including St Anne's Edge Hill, the Assembly Rooms and St Patrick's Chapel. He then visited many other towns, achieving equally dramatic numbers of pledges from all classes and creeds. On his return to Liverpool, 14th September he breakfasted at the Rathbones' in the company of other influential guests.

One wonders how success was measured. Kerrigan, in his fully-researched and comprehensive book on Mathew, critically evaluates success as measured in crude estimates of numbers of pledges "taken". However the *Liverpool Mercury* (1843 page 312) did report a consequent decrease in number of persons brought before the magistrates for drink offences, and the takings of eight "dram shops" went down by £36 a week (*Mercury* page 266). It was further reported that some "crafty publicans, afraid of loosing their unhappy slaves, attempted to interrupt meetings". This later became a regular problem, perhaps an indication of Mathew's effectiveness.

Why was Mathew so well and so widely accepted in Liverpool? Naturally the large Irish immigrant population welcomed him. The Temperance movement and the Liberals, with whom they were associated, were glad to see him (the latter if only because he was in opposition to the

Conservative brewers). Scots, Presbyterians, Nonconformists, all received him. Though Mathew was friendly with Daniel O'Connell he always avoided close support for Irish nationalism, indeed he avoided politics in general. Perhaps his greatest appeal was to philanthropists, such as the Rathbones, and to industrialists. The former saw his work as improving the well-being of the populace, the latter anticipated increased industrial productivity. Burke (*Catholic History of Liverpool*) gives an additional reason for Mathew's second visit to Liverpool. He came "to show his personal appreciation of the work done by the Hibernian Schools under the guidance of the Rathbones, Holts and Hornbys".

In his biography of Father Mathew, Maguire quotes, often at length, letters written by him to the Rathbones in Liverpool. References to the Rathbones are conspicuous by their absence in Winskill's four volume *History of the Temperance Movement*, where Mathew's work is described in detail. In his letters, usually to Mrs Rathbone, Mathew tries to avoid politics and nationalism (Irish home rule) though he touches on the problem in his 1848 letter. He tries to reassure his friends about insurrection in Ireland. "Guilty as our wretched people have been, there was not a conspiracy amongst them to kill the landed gentry". Less reassuring is his next sentence, "the struggle for possession of land was the dire cause of shedding human blood". Mathew does not underplay his own hand when concluding "not a single teetotaller out of the millions (sic) was implicated in the guilt .... the convicts were all whiskey drinkers".

**The Irish Famine and the Rathbones**

The Rathbones, via Father Mathew, played a large part in helping victims of the famine and of Typhus, especially in Cork, during 1847. As Maguire writes in his biography " no friends whom he had known at any period of his career were truer, more generous, or more unwearying and unselfish in their kindness towards him, than the Rathbones".

William Rathbone was always generous and practically-minded. Mathew was known to be weak in his financial accounting. He was regularly accused of making a personal fortune from the sale of temperance medals. These medals were introduced by John Hockins the "Birmingham Blacksmith". Local societies would buy medals for six shillings and sell them for fourteen, for their own funds. In Ireland, Mathew spent much on transport to reach all over the country. However, as Kerrigan points out he did accept free use of carriages from a businessman who subsequently made great profits transporting would-be pledge takers, in great numbers, to attend Mathew's meetings!

When Rathbone arranged for "quantities of breadstuffs" to be brought from America to Ireland, he decided to visit Cork himself, accompanied by his wife and son, to personally watch Mathew's distribution of the aid. This was in April 1847. He was also accompanied by the American ship's captain who had transported the aid. Together they visited the soup kitchens and food depots. Rathbone wanted to see " individual instances of distress". Accordingly, Mathew took his visitors to the first house they came to. Having entered, Mathew came out to say that six of the ten occupants had typhus fever. " Come and see" he said. Only the ship's captain, who said he had no dependants, entered! He declared that the misery he had seen was beyond description. Maguire continues his account "from that moment Theobald Mathew obtained the confidence of William Rathbone". Many years later, in 1863, Rathbone wrote to Maguire, remembering Mathew's "goodness and practical efficiency". Rathbone's trade in breadstuffs with North America is discussed by Lucie Nottingham, who also gives a helpful Rathbone family tree.

The famine in Ireland continued in 1848, and in his July letter to Rathbone, Mathew was both grateful and optimistic "your last remittance. .... from the good people of Boston has been put to good use". Mathew says that he was optimistic about the "many luxuriant fields of potatoes and turnips, from seed I was enabled to distribute". The optimism was short lived. In August he wrote " Dear Mr Rathbone, I regret that the melancholy task of announcing the total destruction of the potato crop....". Mathew admits " in every way I encouraged the propagation of the potatoes, the large sum I received from you I expended on the doomed potato".

**North America**

In 1849 Mathew felt he should honour his longstanding promise to visit America. Having again stayed with his devoted friends the Rathbones he crossed the Atlantic. On his arrival in Boston he was asked to reaffirm his (1842) hatred of slavery. This was a difficult matter for him. Reaffirmation would ensure no visit to, and no pledges from, the Southern States. Which was the lesser evil? He replied that his mission was to "save men from the slavery of intemperance" and declined to enter the slavery debate. This did not totally silence criticism, but he was personally honoured by both houses of Congress and the President declined wine while at a formal dinner held in his honour.

By March 1850 he was in Alabama and wrote to Mrs Rathbone to say that he had "endured much toil and anxiety since (my) departure from your hospitable mansion". He saw the inhabitants of the South as "courteous and affable". The storm, which had been initially raised against him, had abated. He argued that his avoiding condemnation of slavery had enabled him to do good in another field. In May 1850 he reported, again to Mrs Rathbone, from New Orleans that thousands were taking the pledge. He saw this as adequate compensation for any sacrifice he had made concerning his feelings on the slavery question. Is this a personal confession to his correspondent? Is he somehow rationalising his evasion of not condemning slavery?

In this letter he again raises his financial problems " I have avoided any act... influenced by mercenary motives". He closes by saying he finds it difficult to make ends meet. In his next letter July 1850, he replies to Mrs Rathbone from Arkansas thanking her for the " unexpected and unexampled generosity of Mr Rathbone". (Unexpected perhaps, but not totally unsolicited). He goes on to explain why he was so out-of-pocket but adds that he is now enabled to go and preach to the native Indians and save them from their drunkenness.

By October 1850, Mathew writes, again to Mrs Rathbone " You do not appear to approve of my protracted stay in America". (It would be informative to be able to read her letters). He explains that he has been ill and that he was continuing to work for teetotalism and for famine relief. He fears to return because of his creditors expectations. He tells her that he loves her "as a sister " and envies his letter as it will reach the shores of the old country before he does. (England rather than Ireland?). Does he emotionally blackmail his "sister" when he writes that his liabilities "can only be liquidated by my death, an event , which in any case, cannot be far distant"?

His perceptive views on his fellow Irishmen in America may still be relevant to many of us today. He noted that in a land of plenty, in comparison to starving Ireland, "Young Irish....were dying because of tobacco, strong drink, excess fresh meat and overwork".

He spent much of the next year, 1851, in New Orleans and was "acquainted" with the "Swedish Nightingale", Jenny Lind. The latter had a connection with Liverpool. When the Southern Hospital needed money to expand, a deputation was sent to Leeds to ask her to sing in Liverpool which she did on 6th January 1849. £1300 was raised and she was given a silver kettle and stand, a poetic address, and a ward was named after her (Macallister, *History of the Southern Hospital*). Mathew finally left America in November 1851 returning to Ireland via England. He suffered various illnesses, convalescing in Madeira on one occasion. He spent his remaining years in Queenstown, now called Cobh and died there in December 1856.
(Liverpool's Father Nugent followed Mathew, lecturing in America in 1890.)

**Other's opinions**

Eleanor Rathbone, in her biography of her father, the sixth William Rathbone, describes her grandparents, the Rathbones who entertained Mathew. She writes of the political price they paid for such activities, especially their support of Irish Catholic schools in Liverpool. She noted that her grandfather "placed an almost unbounded and implicit reliance" on his wife's judgement and insight into character. Perhaps that is why Father Mathew wrote to Mrs and not Mr Rathbone.

An interesting description of Mathew and his activities in Ireland is given by the journalist and author W. M. Thackeray, who drank his way around Ireland in 1840 and 1842 having been contracted to write a travelogue on the country. After a particularly heavy night on champagne he " came down rather late (with) a slight headache and extreme longing for soda water". He met Mathew over breakfast, but was unable to explain to him the reason for his soda water breakfast, recording " it would have been a confession to a Catholic priest and as a Protestant I am above it". Thackeray had been told "all the fun has gone out of Ireland since Mathew banished the whiskey from it ...meetings (were) no longer gay, but gloomy". Seemingly these were exaggerated reports since Thackeray records that half the population had taken the pledge - presumably this left the other half to join him in copious over-consumption.

Thackeray was clearly impressed by Mathew, describing him as having presence and personality. A handsome honest-looking man of some two and forty years. Mathew had been born 52 years earlier! He did not have "the scowl which darkens the faces of Irish priesthood" ! Thackeray records that Matthew spoke frankly "one would not know if he were a Whig or a Tory, Catholic or Protestant. He had a rare non-partisan approach and the minutest practical knowledge of the diverse social problems of his country and the ways of bettering them". His conversation concerned farming leases, rents, reading and musical societies, never politics. Thackeray concludes that he should be made a Privy Counsellor - if he would honour that body by taking a seat amongst them. This breakfast meeting was concluded by Mathew "taking the ladies of our party to see his burying ground where Protestants and Catholics may lie together without clergymen quarrelling over their coffins".

## Class Issues and Politics

**F E Smith, Lord Birkenhead**

Most Victorian authors agreed that problems due to drunkenness occurred only amongst the working classes. The upper classes could drink to saturation in the safety of their homes and clubs. At times their drunkenness was more than tolerated, it was expected.

If upper class youths were involved in drunken vandalism, this was "high spirits". A case in point was that of F.E. Smith, later Lord Birkenhead and Chancellor of England. His life is detailed in John Campbell's excellent biography. After two years at University College Liverpool, F E as he was known, transferred to Oxford (1891). There, having captained his team at a successful rugby trip to Cambridge, his team was involved in the wrecking of a railway carriage. Compensation cost him £20.The episode had no adverse effect on his career. As a fresh-man he was chosen to speak against the leading Temperance campaigner of the day, at the Oxford Union. Later he became its president.

His subsequent involvement with drink was considerable, politically, professionally and, sadly, personally. These involvements were at local and national levels. From his chambers in Cook Street and later Lord Street, he earned much of his living representing the brewers and publicans at licensing committee sessions. These vested interests opposed any reduction in the number of public house licences. When the closure was inevitable and compensation was on offer, F. E. was there for the benefit of his clients. Politics were closely entwined with the drink trade. The brewers and their publicans were closely allied with the Conservatives. The opposition, the Liberals, were accordingly supported by the Temperance Movement. In Liverpool particularly, religion was an added ingredient. Protestant Ulstermen sided with the Conservatives, Irish Catholics, who wanted home rule for Ireland, with the Liberals. Thus a seemingly unusual alliance was formed between the Catholics and the Teetotallers!

In 1905, the Liverpool licensing committee, ruled by the Conservatives, set a low rate of compensation for public houses that faced closure.

Compensation came from a levy on those pubs that remained. It was believed that a high rate of compensation would have reduced the overall number of pubs and been expensive for those that continued, not to the liking of "The Trade", hence the action of the Conservative majority. The *Liverpool Daily Post* called the Conservative members "friends if not representatives" of "The Trade". The Conservative members sued the editor for criminal libel. Not even F.E. could win the case for them against a popular and upright newspaper editor.

To further curb the effects of drink, public houses' days and hours of opening were restricted. This had an adverse effect on the brewers' and publicans' profits and was thus attractive to Liberals and to the Temperance Movement. The Liberals, however, did support private clubs, their own included, which could sell alcohol, thus bypassing the publicans. There were fewer restrictions on these clubs. In a debate in the House of Commons, F. E. attacked the Liberals' position. The moral high ground had already been prepared for him by his close friend Archibald Salvidge, the doyen of Liverpool politics, who had ensured that all the Liverpool Conservative Working Men's clubs were teetotal, unlike the Liberal ones. F. E. could thus speak from a principled position. It is to be noted that they were "working men's" clubs! F.E. was honest enough to acknowledge class bias in legislation "coercion of the uncellared by the cellared" as he put it. He was referring to wine cellars, not the squalid cellars often associated with the poor in Liverpool. There is a similar quote in the *Daily Post* 10th January 1906 " those who hold the key to their own wine cellars, should not denounce those who have no cellars". Though F. E. claimed to have acted professionally for those opposed to "The Trade" evidence is hard to find.

F. E. came from a conservative background, his beliefs were clear, he constantly espoused the individual's freedom to drink, writing "better England free than England sober". An alternative view had been expressed by the Liberal's Viscount Goschen in 1866, " The Tories are more afraid of the working classes when they think than when they drink". It was considered that the working classes were more likely to combine against the establishment if they were sober, an outcome which was a constant fear of the upper classes. Alcohol was seen as an opium

*1. The Drunkard's Children*

*2. The Drunkard's Children*

*3. Intemperance, Step 5*

*4. Take a Public House*

*5. Intemperance, Step 2*

*6. Death Unmasked*

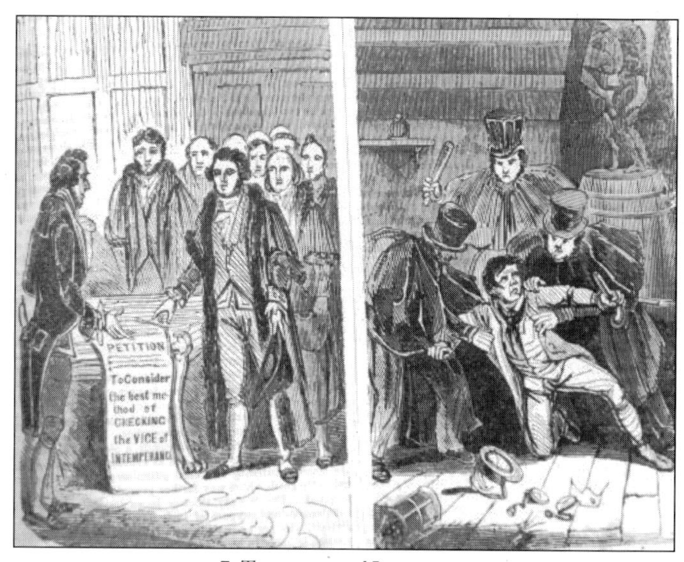


*7. Temperance and Intemperance*

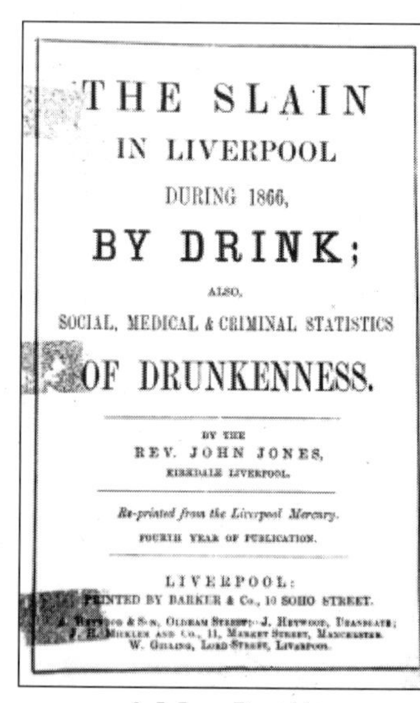

THE SLAIN
IN LIVERPOOL
DURING 1866,
BY DRINK;
ALSO,
SOCIAL, MEDICAL & CRIMINAL STATISTICS
OF DRUNKENNESS.

BY THE
REV. JOHN JONES,
KIRKDALE LIVERPOOL.

*Re-printed from the Liverpool Mercury.*
FOURTH YEAR OF PUBLICATION.

LIVERPOOL:
PRINTED BY BARKER & Co., 10 SOHO STREET.
[illegible] & Son, Oldham Street; J. Heywood, Deansgate;
J. H. Mickles and Co., 11, Market Street, Manchester.
W. Gilling, Lord Street, Liverpool.

*8. J. Jones Pamphlet*

*9. Rev R. H. Lundie*

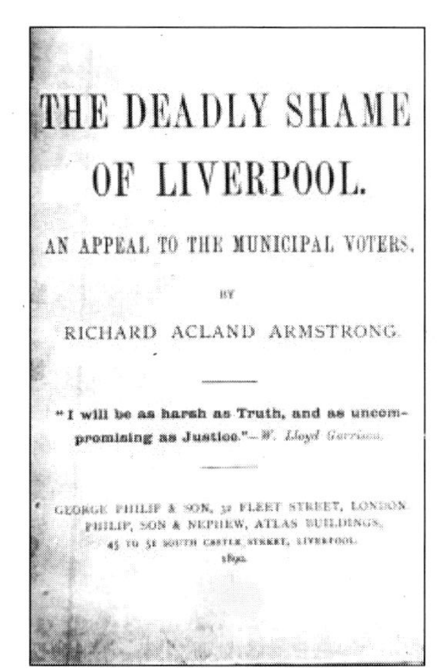

THE DEADLY SHAME
OF LIVERPOOL.

AN APPEAL TO THE MUNICIPAL VOTERS.

BY

RICHARD ACLAND ARMSTRONG.

"I will be as harsh as Truth, and as uncompromising as Justice."—*W. Lloyd Garrison.*

GEORGE PHILIP & SON, 32 FLEET STREET, LONDON.
PHILIP, SON & NEPHEW, ATLAS BUILDINGS,
45 TO 51 SOUTH CASTLE STREET, LIVERPOOL.
1892.

10. *Armstrong's first pamphlet*

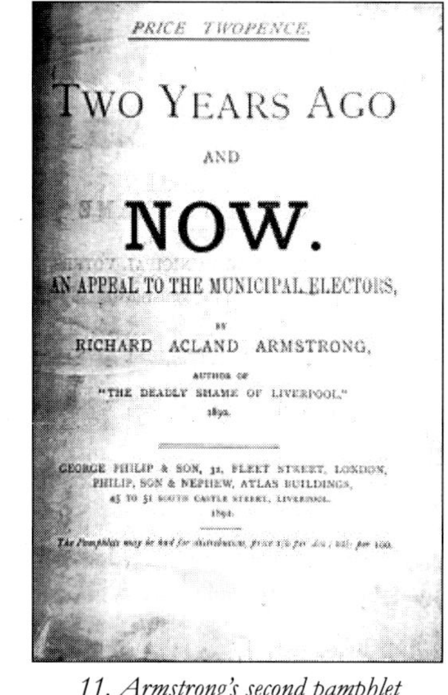

*PRICE TWOPENCE.*

TWO YEARS AGO
AND
NOW.

AN APPEAL TO THE MUNICIPAL ELECTORS,

BY

RICHARD ACLAND ARMSTRONG,

AUTHOR OF
"THE DEADLY SHAME OF LIVERPOOL,"
1892.

GEORGE PHILIP & SON, 32, FLEET STREET, LONDON,
PHILIP, SON & NEPHEW, ATLAS BUILDINGS,
45 TO 51 SOUTH CASTLE STREET, LIVERPOOL.
1894.

11. *Armstrong's second pamphlet*

12. *Canon A. Hume*

13. *John Finch*

14. *Thomas Swindlehurst*

*15. Hope Hall*

HONOURABLE MENTION FOR GOOD QUALITY,
INTERNATIONAL EXHIBITION, 1862.

PASSOVER OR SACRAMENTAL WINE.
Unfermented and Unintoxicating; prepared from the finest Continental grapes, and preserved "in vacuo" at the suggestion and under the direction of Dr. F. R. Lees, by FRANK WRIGHT, Chemist, Kensington, London.

This wine has now stood the test of nine years' use by the Temperance Churches, and has received the sanction and approval of all the principal leaders in the movement. Dr. F. R. Lees, F.S.A.; Dr. Gale, Rector of Treborough, H. Mudge, Esq., M.R.C.S.; The Rev. Dr. Kirk, the Rev. Evan Lewis, M.A., the Rev. Jabez Burns, D.D., and many others have kindly expressed their warm approbation of its merits and their desire for its general adoption. Price 2s per bottle, half bottles 1s 2d.

AGENT FOR LIVERPOOL—
J. LAMONT, CONFECTIONER, 199, LONDON ROAD.
*or may be had at the office of this paper, 7, Clayton Square.*

*16. Sacramental Wine*

17. *Liverpool Medical Institution & Hope Hall*

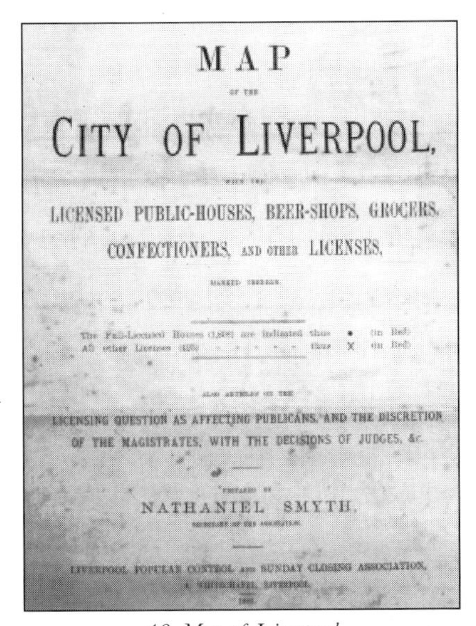

MAP

CITY OF LIVERPOOL,

LICENSED PUBLIC-HOUSES, BEER-SHOPS, GROCERS,

CONFECTIONERS, AND OTHER LICENSES,

LICENSING QUESTION AS AFFECTING PUBLICANS, AND THE DISCRETION OF THE MAGISTRATES, WITH THE DECISIONS OF JUDGES, &c.

NATHANIEL SMYTH,

LIVERPOOL POPULAR CONTROL AND SUNDAY CLOSING ASSOCIATION,

18. *Map of Liverpool*

THE LIVERPOOL

Social Reformer:

THE ORGAN OF THE TEMPERANCE MOVEMENT.

No. 1. OCTOBER 1st, 1871. Price 1d.

CONTENTS.



TO OUR READERS AND FRIENDS.

In bringing out the little monthly serial now in your hands, the editors venture to believe they are supplying a want which has long been felt by an important section of society in Liverpool.

The Temperance movement has assumed such a position in the town, and taken such a hold upon large masses of the community, that the time has arrived when some means for the interchange of opinion, and imparting information, on the Temperance question of all denominations, and other leading people, in the confident hope that a monthly statement of the successful efforts made by the friends of temperance to reform society, by counteracting the baneful influence of the liquor traffic, may gradually win respect for our movement, where it does not convert to our principles.

The editors appeal to all friends of temperance to help on the circulation of the "*Liverpool Social Reformer*." Every teetotaller should buy a copy monthly, and every temperance society should take a given

*19. Social Reformer, First Issue*

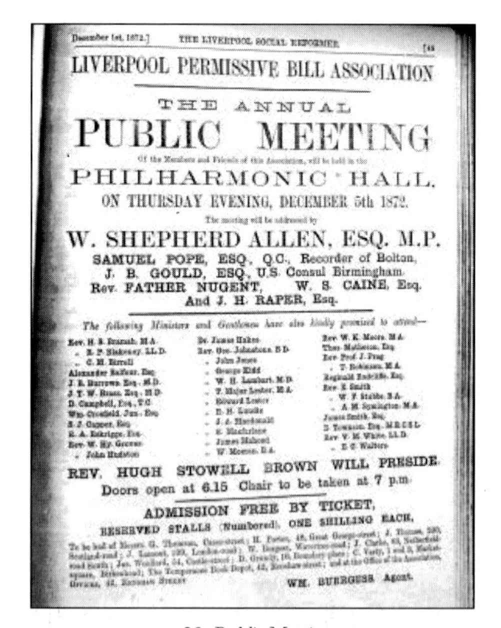

December 1st, 1872.] THE LIVERPOOL SOCIAL REFORMER. [41

LIVERPOOL PERMISSIVE BILL ASSOCIATION

THE ANNUAL

PUBLIC MEETING

Of the Members and Friends of this Association, will be held in the

PHILHARMONIC HALL,

ON THURSDAY EVENING, DECEMBER 5th 1872.

The meeting will be addressed by

W. SHEPHERD ALLEN, ESQ. M.P.

SAMUEL POPE, ESQ., Q.C., Recorder of Bolton,

J. B. GOULD, ESQ., U.S. Consul Birmingham,

Rev. FATHER NUGENT, W. S. CAINE, Esq.

And J. H. RAPER, Esq.

*The following Ministers and Gentlemen have also kindly promised to attend—*

| | | |
|---|---|---|
| Rev. H. S. [illegible], M.A. | Dr. James Hakes | Rev. W. K. Moore, M.A. |
| „ [illegible], LL.D. | Rev. Geo. Johnstone, B.D. | Thos. Matheson, Esq. |
| „ C. M. [illegible] | „ John Jones | Rev. Prof. J. [illegible] |
| Alexander Balfour, Esq. | „ George Kidd | „ T. Robinson, M.A. |
| J. R. [illegible], Esq., M.D. | „ W. H. Lambert, M.D. | Reginald Radcliffe, Esq. |
| J. T. W. [illegible], Esq., M.D. | „ T. Major Lester, M.A. | Rev. E. Smith |
| D. Campbell, Esq., T.C. | „ Edward Lester | „ W. F. [illegible], B.A. |
| Wm. Crosfield, Jun., Esq. | „ [illegible] | „ A. M. Symington, M.A. |
| [illegible], Esq. | „ J. A. [illegible] | James Smith, Esq. |
| [illegible], Esq. | „ [illegible] | [illegible], Esq., M.R.C.S.L. |
| Rev. W. Hy. [illegible] | „ James Mahood | Rev. V. M. White, LL.D. |
| „ John [illegible] | „ W. [illegible], B.A. | „ E. C. Walters |

REV. HUGH STOWELL BROWN WILL PRESIDE.

Doors open at 6.15 Chair to be taken at 7 p.m.

ADMISSION FREE BY TICKET,

RESERVED STALLS (Numbered), ONE SHILLING EACH,

To be had of Messrs. G. Thomson, [illegible]; H. [illegible], 48, Great George-street; [illegible]

WM. BURGESS Agent.

*20. Public Meeting*

of the people. These views are discussed by Andrew Barr in his most interesting and readable book *Drink an Informal Social History*.

Smith enjoyed huge and rapid success in Parliament and then in the Cabinet, he was a brilliant debater. However his own excessive drinking adversely affected him physically, mentally, socially and professionally. Alcoholic amnesia caused him to apologise in writing for not attending a meeting - a meeting at which he had brilliantly spoken the previous evening! When a Liberal MP claimed that not a few MPs were in grave danger of falling victim to the evil (drink) F. E. sarcastically thanked him for not naming them! In 1921, F. E. wagered Lord Beaverbrook £1000 that he could stay abstinent for the year. He returned to drinking in December feeling that the treaty he had just negotiated with Ireland was worth this price!

John Campbell's book makes fascinating reading, all 918 pages! F. E.'s many and varied contributions to improve society by his work as a politician and lawyer are fully discussed. He was a highly successful reformer. The above, possibly negative, account covers only one facet of his life.

**H K Aspinall**

H. K. Aspinall was a Conservative brewer and public house owner in Birkenhead. As chairman of the Mersey Ferry committee he made the bylaw of a 40 shilling penalty for jumping on or off the boat. He himself was the first to be fined in the courts for the offence. When he was precluded from sitting as a magistrate during licensing sessions he protested "since brewers are prohibited as interested parties, surely common fairness would suggest that rabid opponents of the trade should be excluded on the same principle". He ironically added that would-be reformers might not stop at closing the working man's hotel on Sunday. They would soon want people to hand over each weekend, to the head constable, the keys to their wine cellars.

Aspinall does not describe visiting his own pubs, he imbibes at a higher level. He recalls how he thanked William Inman for his hospitality aboard the ship *City of Chester* on its trial run. He recalls "drinking good liquor ad. lib." he adds that the White Star Line "has always excelled in the victualling department". Another who enjoyed drinking aboard was F. E. Smith, a regular guest on the palatial yacht *Liberty*, owned by the West Toxteth MP Robert Houston, known in Liverpool as the Robber Baron, an unscrupulous pirate with his own steamship in South American waters (John Campbell).

Aspinall concedes that there might be drink-related problems in Liverpool, but berates reformers for being antidemocratic. He feels their legislation concerns the minority, the drunkards, thus adversely affecting the rights of the majority, the drinkers. Brewers, he claims, are "highly respectable, philanthropic, liberal minded, gentlemen". He believes that the solution to drunkenness is in improved sanitary and economic conditions, not in Acts of Parliament. His conclusion, "moderation", is reminiscent of Yates' wine lodge motto "moderation is true temperance" (Yates, 1984).

**Clark Aspinall**

Quite different, as regards attitude towards drinking, was Clark Aspinall whose biography was written by W. Lewin. Many generations of Aspinalls were active in Liverpool society and, according to the book, seem to have been quite a rum bunch, or perhaps just men of their time. In the days of the early Aspinalls, at election time, "drunkenness was supreme for two or three weeks. The price of a vote was anything from a quart of ale to £100 or more".

H. K. Aspinall (above) was Clark Aspinall's second cousin. Clark's brother was Recorder of Liverpool. Clark himself was a magistrate in Wirral and in Liverpool but his main work was as Coroner in Liverpool. His biography relates his witticisms aimed at people brought before him for drunk and disorderly behaviour, a charge which seemed to be a speciality for him. His wit was often aimed at offenders who cited their large dependent families as a reason for obtaining leniency. One case, a man of 92, was accused of being drunk and disorderly. He offered as an excuse the fact that he was an orphan. He was discharged. This may have been better than medical referral. About that time Dr. R. Saundby, Professor of Medicine at Birmingham University, was advocating "mechanical restraint.....heroic doses of chloral.....strychnine etc", for elderly alcoholics.

Lewin gives separate chapters to Clark's opinions, personality and characteristics. He had definite opinions, women should remain in their home, the Church of England should stay low and Catholicism was a threat. He was an advocate of the use of the lash. He was keen on hard labour in prison which had to be disagreeable and monotonous e.g. oakum picking and the treadmill. He did not approve of the usual treatment of drunks in court "five shillings and costs", he wanted something more severe, imprisonment. On the other hand he did much philanthropic work and supported with time and money many charities. He was active in the temperance movement having taken the pledge himself. One feels he did not get on with his cousin H. K. calling him "Mr Brewer Aspinall".

**W B Forwood**

Sir W. B. Forwood, Mayor of Liverpool in 1880 and member of various licensing benches, described his contribution to Liverpool life between 1860 and 1910 in his autobiography. As Mayor he had shown his moderation by refusing the offer of a Gattling Gun, "grand things for clearing the streets" - of Fenians (Irish Republicans).

He seemed content with progress made against drunkenness during his time. Though Liverpool was always "liberal and generous in her charities" he admitted there had been "an utter failure to realise the social degradation in which so many of her people lived". He believed one reason was "the town had been flooded with licensed public houses when the justices advocated a free license system". Their action had been in the hope that an excess of outlets would close many of the gin palaces and other outlets. Unsurprisingly the reverse occurred, there was more intemperance. He recalls how the London *Times* chided Liverpool's leading inhabitants who were negligent of their duties as citizens. As a licensing magistrate, he witnessed the crusade led by Alex Balfour, the Rev Dr. Lundie, Sam Smith and Rev Charles Garrett, (whom he called the great apostle of temperance, not Mathew ) against the licensing systems. He concluded that after a long fierce struggle the streets of Liverpool had been purified, a quarter of the public houses had been closed in his time .

**Samuel Smith**

Samuel Smith published his views on his life's work in 1903. He had come to Liverpool from Scotland fifty years earlier to work in the cotton trade and found his place with other Scottish Presbyterian social reformers. Much of his autobiography is devoted to his account of his work to improve the life of destitute children and their drunken parents by offering them practical help and by attacking the cause as he saw it of their woes, "The Trade".

He gives a vivid description of the problems he encountered, "women … hand to hand fights…. children maimed by drunken parents ….people in rags….drink shops took thousands of pounds…. fortunes made by publicans…brewers left millions". One dramatic solution was simply to remove these waifs to a "better" life in Canada. Smith worked with his friend Alex Balfour M P, " who had the honour of starting the emigration". Four thousand in all, of whom 95% did "well". No mention is made of any involvement by Father Nugent.

However Smith did realise that the real solution lay in a change in behaviour in Liverpool. He saw himself as a " visionary who tried to awaken public opinion", by speeches and letters to the papers. No mention of Shimmin. He had little confidence in the press "many of our newspapers had Romish Sub-editors …. some trained by a Jesuit college employed to furnish pressmen for English papers".

He saw that there had to be an alternative to the public house for nourishment, company and entertainment. He set about providing practical alternatives. His American connections, led him to invite the American evangelists Sankey and Moody to Liverpool in 1875 . " We built the Victoria Hall …. 8 to 10,000 people, night after night ...the drunken became sober". At one of Moody's meetings it was pointed out that dockers had nowhere to eat, save public houses. This led to the formation of the British Workman Public House Company, which provided "tea, coffee and solid food". The movement had 80 houses in Liverpool serving 20,000 meals a day and later spread to other parts of England and Scotland. Smith reasonably concluded "nothing has done more to make temperance easy among the working classes" (This movement is later described in more detail).

Evening entertainment was his next venture. When the Coliseum in Paradise Street closed, ("30 or 40 people were trodden to death"), Smith took the theatre and arranged "wholesome and innocent amusements on temperance lines for the poor degraded population of the lowest stratum". On Sundays there was the added inducement of a loaf of bread "for the debris of our social system, men and women who had drunk themselves to rags". He tells us between 15 and 20,000 took the temperance pledge. No mention of other pledge takers, one begins to feel he did everything himself, no others were working in the same fields. Above the Coliseum there was a Sunday school, a thousand children in the room with 60 teachers. Smith wanted to educate " all Protestant children" and condemned those who used schools "to destroy the principles of the Reformation…restore Roman doctrines…. priest craft".

Smith accurately saw the source of drunkenness. "The drink trade was the curse of the town, Liverpool was a worshipper of the great Goddess beer. It was entrenched in the town council and magistracy. Even the watch committee which controlled the police, was dominated by the drink trade". Smith blamed both parties, his own, the Liberals, who had given out licences freely, and the Conservatives who would not give them up.

Smith writes "Temperance and thrift go along with clean and wholesome dwellings . Drunkenness causes a vast infant mortality and premature death". He recalls "great sanitary reform had been carried through …the worst property destroyed. Liverpool is stretching out long arms into the country…electric tramways". He wanted all unused building land to be taxed, so that new suburbs could be built where no public houses were allowed. Parliament Field was built with such restrictions. "Toxteth is a striking example of keeping out the liquor trade ….. sale of intoxicating liquor prohibited …. under prohibition …. 200 streets, 12,000 houses, 60,000 population without a public house". In 1891 death rates of 10 to 12 per thousand occurred in such districts. Where public houses abounded, the rate was 41. Smith does not demonstrate cause and effect between drinking and death-rates, nor does he contemplate the use of the trams by drinkers escaping from their dry estates. In the 1960s, residents of the newly-built Kirby had to travel back to Liverpool town-centre to find sufficient pubs! Enforced geographical prohibition is later discussed.

Smith concludes his biography, with a collection of his own speeches. As a self-confessed "infamous slave driver", he paid labourers 3/6 (17p) a day, six days a week, (£1. 05p a week). If he paid six shillings (30p) a day "Irish and other Europeans would crowd in". A three day working week would result, (90p a week). Other speeches condemned newspapers for publishing divorce case details since "It is impossible to keep the newspaper out of the hands of children and domestic servants".

This is all Smith's own, mature, considered opinion, forthrightly expressed. He would have been an interesting man to work with, or for. Munro and Sim, in their *Merseyside Scots*, place his contribution highly amongst those of his countrymen.

**William Lever, geographical prohibition**

Temperance workers relied on the persuasive power of their oratory and perhaps a little mass hysteria to make people want to abstain of their own volition. The potential drinker was still in charge of his or her subsequent behaviour, it was their decision, albeit taken under various pressures. They were ultimately in charge of their subsequent drinking habits. But there were other ways. External authorities could attempt to enforce abstinence, or at least make it more difficult for the drinker to indulge. These coercions could be at a national or at a local level.

*Increase price by raising duty paid on beer and spirits, (national government ).*
*Reduce number of outlets e.g. pubs and off-licences, (local magistrates).*
*Reduce alcoholic strength e.g. beer only licences, (local magistrates).*
*Reduce opening hours and days, (local and national).*
*Prohibit pubs and off-licences in whole areas.*

The last mentioned is of local interest. The licensing magistrates could, in theory, instigate geographical prohibition to some extent, but the licensing bench was often under great pressure from "The Trade" and their lawyers and from the voters in elections, that is if they actually wanted to make any reductions in outlets - which was often doubted. Again there was another way.

Benevolent factory owners, for the very best of motives, had begun to create new towns and garden suburbs. A famous pioneer in this movement was Titus Salt who built Saltaire (1853-63). Salt insisted that the town be teetotal, no pubs in his Utopia!

More locally, William Lever built Port Sunlight soap factory and village. He too ruled that there be no drink outlets though he did provide many facilities for the leisure time of his workers e.g. a men's social club and a village inn. He encouraged societies e.g. dining club, bowling club, the British Women's Temperance Society (Port Sunlight branch), and the Young People's Temperance League. Perhaps he should have paid more attention to men's temperance because objection was raised to the Bridge Inns being unlicensed. Lever tolerated discussion, so organised a referendum on the matter. He tried to safeguard his position by requiring that 75% be in favour of the inn's obtaining a licence. He also stipulated that women could vote, probably seeing this as a further safeguard. He still lost, 80% voted for the licensing of the inn! (See S. Meacham's account).

Lever was a capitalist. It was certainly in his own and in his business's interest to have a sober workforce, just as it was in the interest of his workers not to endure the unhappiness excess drinking brought. Lever wanted to make a profit and he was prepared to share these profits, but only in his own way. "You are going to receive £8 each .....spend it in the public house....have a good spree......it will not do you much good if you send it down your throats in the form of bottles of whisky..... if you leave this money with me I shall use it to provide you with nice houses, comfortable homes and healthy recreation". The sting was in the tale. "I am disposed to allow profit-sharing under no other form" (S. Meacham).

Lever was later involved in finding other ways to enforce temperance on an unwilling workforce, this time at a national level. During the 1914-

18 war Lloyd George set up the Central Control Board (liquor traffic) to "control the sale and supply of intoxicating liquor for the successful prosecution of the war" The board introduced:

*Restriction in licensing hours, open 12-2.30pm and 6-9 pm.*
*Reduction in proof strength of spirits.*
*Reduction in off-licence sales.*
*Rule on "no treating", to avoid additional rounds of drinks.*
*Closure of public houses which were near certain factories.*

Barr, in his *Drink an Informal Social History*, describes the operation of the no treating rule, "a workman in Liverpool was given three months hard labour for treating a friend and a husband in Bristol who was fined for buying his wife a drink".

A similar but earlier model village had been set up by William Wilson in Brombrough in 1854 known as Price's Village. There was no such person as Price. The firm's history describes how the workers' social needs were met; subsidised houses, Co-op store, free school, hospital, sports, societies, pensions and profit-sharing. No mention of any public house.

Rev. R. H. Lundie, in 1880, ironically wrote that when pubs no longer made a profit "remove them to the suburbs where Welsh builders are raising new streets by the score". Brewer's capital was obtained for corner sites, even if there were enough pubs already. The popularity of corner sites is emphasised by Freddy O'Connor in his *A Pub on Every Corner*". If the licence wasn't given, re-application should be made until "a pliable set of justices" was found. In this way, "degradation" spreads to the suburbs.

By 1895 Lundie, in his biography of his friend Alexander Balfour, wrote more kindly of Welsh builders. He describes the work of Mr John Roberts MP for Flintshire who prohibited the erection of public houses on the large estates that he was building in Liverpool. Lundie's account of his conversations with Balfour show how closely some religious and political figures worked together in the temperance cause.

**Welsh Builders and Prohibition**

Welsh builders formed a distinct group on Merseyside, which contributed greatly to developments on both sides of the river. J.R. Jones in *The Welsh Builder on Merseyside*, gives biographical details of over 400 individual builders and lists the roads and estates they developed. Most had emigrated from Anglesey, usually by ship, but occasionally walking to Liverpool. They were generous in their support of local hospitals, churches and chapels. They were, as Picton describes them, "an industrious, steady and sober race".

Jones' book reports that David Roberts, Son (John) and Co. bought land in the Princes Park area (now Princes Road) which included Parliament Fields, from the Earl Sefton, in about 1864. "On this estate there is not a single public house, because of the restrictive covenant inserted in the conveyances and agreed to by the builders, and this covenant is in force today. This was the pioneer firm to insert such restrictive covenants against selling intoxicating liquors and has resulted in a considerable portion of Liverpool being free of public houses. It should always be remembered that the firm of David Roberts played an important part in thus shaping public policy in relation to the welfare of town areas".

However Jones also writes of Owen Elias who arrived in Liverpool shortly before 1820. He built in Kirkdale, Walton, Everton, Cabbage Hall, West Derby and Toxteth Park. His firm was "responsible also for one noteworthy innovation. Finding that the Justices granted licences to the newly-formed districts and that in the presence of a public house at a street corner caused the neighbourhood to deteriorate, the Welsh builders disposed of the menace by introducing a new condition into their terms of sale. If the prohibition were dictated entirely by business considerations it proved to be based on sound wisdom. If it were prompted by reasons of conscience, it proved as beneficial in operation as it was good in motive".

William Jones served on Bootle Council for "40 years" and applied his temperance principles on the licensing bench and also in his business activity. He built in Toxteth Park and Orrell and demolished Bootle Hall to develop a large estate. However he refused to sell even a single yard for public house development, even when offered "an attractive price".

Occasionally some Welsh builders were more pliable. The six Lewis Brothers of Cemaes, Anglesey "built public houses, opened them, obtained licences for them and then sold the premises". These men also kept two pawnshops and racehorses! Not typical of their fellow countrymen.

Lilian Shiman, in her discussion of abstinent towns, writes "The area called Toxteth Park was said to be the largest prohibition area in England, with a population of 50,000….".

Today we regularly read of a form of geographical prohibition. Local Authorities forbid the drinking of alcohol on various streets or areas of a town. Further, Local Councils will, from November 2005, take to themselves, from the Magistrates, the responsibility for issuing liquor licences. They intend to introduce saturation zones where they consider there are already sufficient outlets and where no more are required. (*Daily Telegraph* Nov 29th 2004). Time will tell if these intentions come to pass. It seems more likely that the Councils will allow longer and longer opening hours for public houses. "The Trade" would not wish to extend hours unless it made greater profits, achieved by selling yet more alcohol.

**Nathaniel Hawthorne**

An outsider's view of Liverpool's problems was given by the author Nathaniel Hawthorne, American consul in Liverpool in the 1850s, in his *Our Old Home,* see also James O'Donald Mays' *Mr. Hawthorne goes to England.* Hawthorne worked from a shabby smoke-stained office in the city, but lived in superior accommodation in Rock Park, Birkenhead. He disliked Liverpool as a place of residence recording that it was "the most convenient and admirable point to get away from". He complained about his clientele "Beggardly and piratical-looking scoundrels, the scum of every maritime nation".

Though his work caused him to socialise with the upper classes he saw this as an "encumbrance". He preferred to "turn aside from the prosperous thoroughfares and enter Dickens' grimiest precincts". He found many such in Liverpool. Drunkenness was ever present. "Ragged children come (to spirit vaults) with old shaving mugs or broken-nosed teapots to get a little poison or madness for their parents". In the pubs he saw women who were "inconceivably sluttish" and men who were continually drunk.

He is surprisingly charitable towards this unattractive behaviour. He will not condemn them "till I had some better consolation to offer....to lift them a little way out of the smothering squalor of both their outward and interior life". He recognised the need for practical and spiritual improvement. However he is unconvinced of the beneficial effects of the work of temperance reformers. In *Our Old Home* he gives critical accounts of Mayoral banquets in Liverpool and London. Life in these quarters is quite different but excessive drinking is again the norm.

## Alternatives to Drink

**Edwin A. Pratt - Defender of the Trade**

A defence of the licensed trade was attempted by Pratt, a journalist and author, who had previously published his study of Scandinavian licensing laws, a work that was well reviewed e.g. in the *Catholic* and *Church Times*. Pratt saw alcohol as having become a scapegoat for all of society's ills, part of a continuum which in the past had included mediaeval plagues, Spanish Protestants, the Catholic mass and dancing.

In his book *The Licensed Trade* he argues against the prohibitionist's case. He reverses the usual cause and effect argument. "To victims of social or domestic conditions the public house is an alternative to squalid tenements". In his view the public house is "the only place where they can be sure of warmth shelter and comfort". It has to be admitted there was much truth in that assertion, regrettably. He quotes Father Bernard Vaughan of Liverpool. "All this poverty due to drink. Nonsense. The drink upset (the poor) because they had no food to take with it". Vaughan defended a man's right to buy beer, adding "Fie upon those who prevented the poor from getting a drink, when they emptied the decanter themselves".

As an apologist for the trade he gives a rather slanted view of the "Free Trade in Beer" Acts of Parliament (1829-69). He, not unreasonably, singles out Liverpool police and magistrates for particular criticism in allowing "Fifty new beer shops every day for several weeks in cellars and other unfit premises". He preferred the " Management system - first established in Liverpool ". He continues to praise Liverpool's pubs wherein he saw "Large plates of hot pot for two pence, with free pickles" available for dock labourers. Perhaps he was recognising the inroads made by non-licensed cafes which spread from the docklands of Liverpool. He attacked all "The Trade's" opposition including private clubs which sold alcohol, teetotal drinks such as tea and coffee, and foreign beers and lagers.

He loses his reader's sympathy when he enters the field of Eugenics. He believes the weakest in society should "go to the wall". These unfortunates include lunatics, the weak-minded, consumptives, epileptics, as well as drunkards. “The world is better for their disappearance”. He quotes Dr. G A A Reid in support, who believes diseases and drunkenness “weed out the weak”, leaving the “race strong”. A limit to the “output of children by drunken parents” was advocated without mentioning how this was to be achieved. Pratt felt “Nature’s method, the elimination of the drunkard” was preferable to prohibition, which denied drink to those who could handle it. One might conclude that Edwin A Pratt should be styled Edwin, a pratt.

**Thomas Cook’s first tour, (Liverpool 1845)**

For the poor in cities, outings to the countryside or seaside brought pleasant, if temporary, relief from the squalor of town life. Such outings were often organised by religious societies or churches, perhaps to reward regular attenders. The only happy day in the life of the heroine of *Her Benny* and her brother was the outing across the Mersey to Eastham woods, a popular trip in those days.

Thomas Cook (1808-1899) may be considered to be the inventor of modern tourism, or at least he was its greatest developer and personal conductor on tours. His life and work are described by Piers Brendon (1981). Cook was a printer and Baptist preacher whose passion for the temperance cause may have become an obsession, perhaps to the detriment of his family and business life. Cook had taken the pledge in 1833, but only for strong spirits, not ale. By 1836 he was a total abstainer and enforced the same on his workers. He saw drink as the “the route of nearly all the evils afflicting early Victorian England”.

Living during the time of rapid development of the railway system, he realised that this means of transport could be used to advance his mission. Days out or excursions could be pleasant alternatives to the alehouse and probably more enjoyable than temperance meetings. It would be a great attraction for potential new recruits. He organised various social occasions for the temperance movement and in 1841 he began to arrange day trips by train from various Midlands towns. Large numbers of temperance supporters, travelling from different places, would all meet for a day together. They would parade in great numbers, perhaps to impress potential converts. They could demonstrate how pleasant life could be without drink. They had bands, banners, games, dancing but all in a temperance setting. Railway managers, who tended to see trains merely as a timetabled means of transport, were persuaded by Cook (and perhaps realising possible profits) to agree to special rates and special trains. Until 1845 these were purely temperance events. However they proved so successful that Cook decided to make it his main business.

This was to be more successful than his other ventures. He had published a wide variety of journals and books, the temperance ones did not do well though he had issued half a million temperance tracts. He moved to Leicester where 40% of all church attenders were, like him, Baptists and because Leicester had good railway connections all over the country. He opened two temperance hotels and was most active in the teetotal movement, exchanging ideas with Father Mathew. One of his less successful activities was to open a temperance club in Fleet Street, London as Brendon puts it "undoubtedly a triumph of hope over experience".

Cook's first professional tour (as opposed to temperance excursions) was to Liverpool, in the summer of 1845. He had previously explored the route and prepared a handbook. Tickets for Liverpool sold out within a few days and a black market existed to buy them. Cook's handbook contained details of places of interest and warnings. He wrote about the "Blackguards who are in the habit of blocking the gateway of (Lime street) station". This was to try to enforce their choice of accommodation on visitors. A similar reception was afforded ferry passengers arriving at New Brighton for a holiday. Their cases were seized by local lads who ran with them to their family's boarding house. (A. E. Laskier, oral history).

Cook personally lead his excursionists to the top of Snowdon, if only to demonstrate that whisky was not obligatory for such exertion. Interestingly, he could find only one English-speaking guide to take his tourists around Caernarvon. The Leicester press praised the tour and within a couple of weeks Cook had arranged a return to Liverpool. In1874 a Cook's office opened in Liverpool.

In 1973 a pub in Leicester was named after Thomas Cook, hardly appropriately. In Liverpool there have recently been two public houses named after Dr. Duncan (Medical Officer of Health). One wonders if these gentlemen would have agreed to the appropriation of their names for these premises. A national chain of public houses has a "policy of respecting local history (which) sadly backfired at Saltaire, where they unwittingly upset locals by naming their new pub after the town's teetotal founder, Sir Titus Salt". (*Times* newspaper,18th Oct 2004).

Liverpool, Manchester and Warrington Temperance members enjoyed a day trip by train to Overton near Chester 1858 (*Illustrated London News* 19th June p 601). But such excursions were not the sole prerogative of teetotal societies. In 1841 a Birmingham publican organised railway excursions for his customers. In 1904 Bass brewery organised one of its four-yearly day excursions to Liverpool, from Burton on Trent. Many hundreds of passengers were transported in seventeen trains, all leaving at ten-minute intervals from 4am.The reprint of Bass' handbook, prepared this journey, makes fascinating reading in its descriptions of entertainments available in Liverpool and New Brighton at that time. The various public houses and cafes which sold Bass were clearly noted, but so were 20 cocoa-rooms of The British Workman's Public House Company, together with 3 of J. G. Spraggs.

A more grisley railway excursion took place in 1856 when "incessant" trains from all over the country, including Liverpool, transported people to Stafford to witness the hanging of Dr. W. Palmer, who had murdered 14 people (see Thomas Boyle's description).

# Medical Views on Intemperance

The physical and mental complications of excessive drinking were widespread in the populace and doctors were called upon to treat them. Alcohol could adversely affect almost every organ in the body. Effects might be acute, e.g. drunken stupor or physical injuries received in accidents or fights, or chronic such as liver disease, mental changers etc. Liverpool was the first authority to appoint a medical officer of health, Dr. W. H. Duncan in 1847. What now is termed Public Health was then included in "sanitation" (See Morris and Ashton, 2002).

Today consideration is given to the effects of drink on an individual's health and behaviour as it affects society. In Victorian times the focus was on the effect of drink on an entire section of the population, the working class. It was seen as a moral issue. They might not be able to avoid cholera, typhus, typhoid, TB etc but they were expected to behave and not get drunk. Occasionally the debilitating effects of drink, leading to increased susceptibility to infectious disease was considered. In the upper classes an individual's illness due to drink might be commented on, e.g. gout. A drunken workforce was not good for industry nor did drunken soldiers make an effective army. Some in authority feared drink could lead to insurrection' however others thought it might induce acquiescence.

The Liverpool Central Relief and Charity Organisation Society, in attempting to fulfil their remit, gave in their annual reports, examples of undeserving cases. Nearly all these cases had an abuse of alcohol as the underlying reason for their problems. Consequently they received no charity (W.Grisewood, long serving Secretary). The sad concept of the undeserving poor has been discussed in detail by Anthony Miller in his *Poverty Deserved? Relieving the Poor in Victorian Liverpool*. The neglected wife and children of a supposed drinker are rejected and receive no support.

**Dr. Duncan (The first Medical Officer of Health)**

The medical reports provided by the medical officers of health in Liverpool provide interesting reading. Duncan's report for the year 1859

*21. Thomastown House*

*22. Theobald Mathew*

23. *William Rathbone*

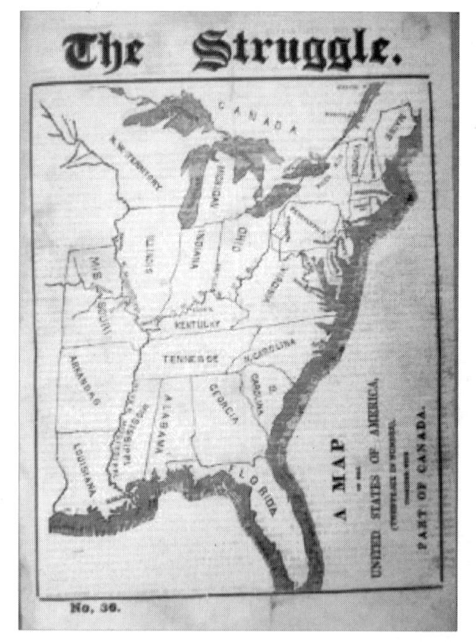


24. *Map of U.S.A.*

*25. H. K. Aspinall*

*26. Clark Aspinall*

*27. W. B. Forewood*

*28. Samuel Smith*

*29. Thomas Cook*

*30. Temperance outing to Chester*

*31. Dr. E. W. Hope*

*32. Dr. W. S. Trench*

*34. Dr. John Hay*

*33. Dr. Francis Vacher*

*35. Cardinal Manning*

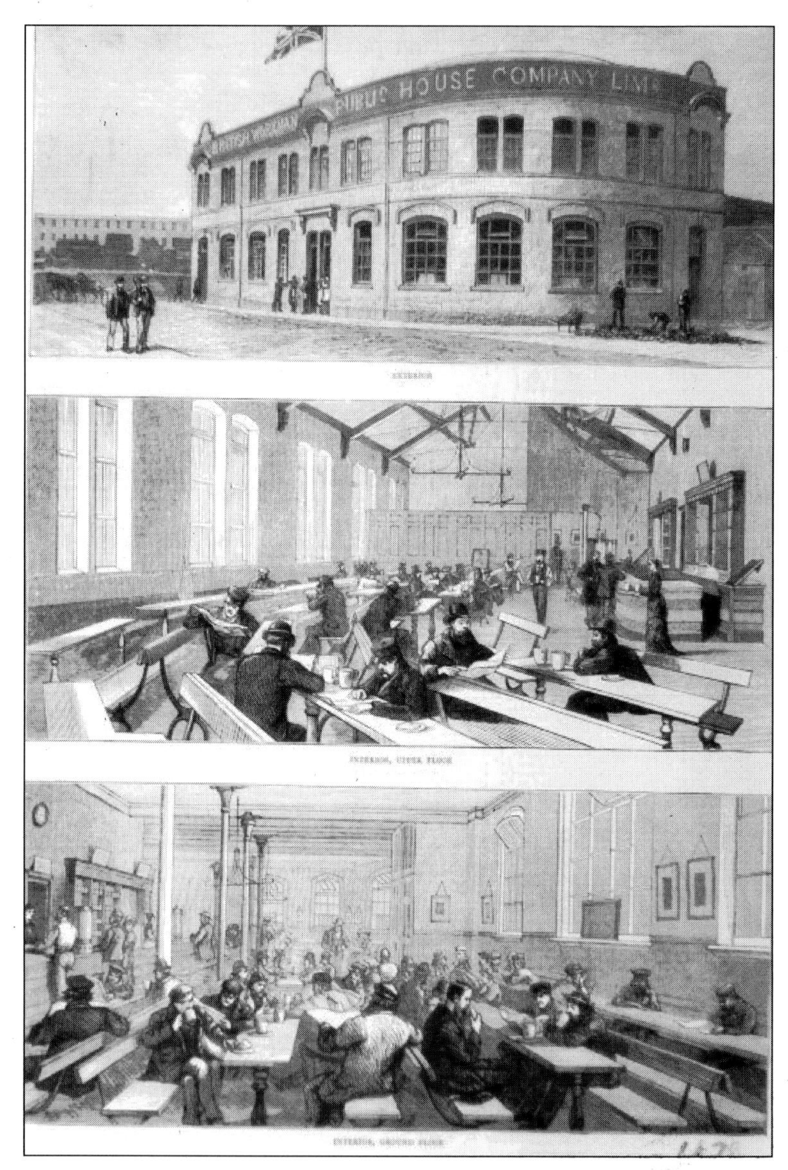


*36. British Workman's Coffee Tavern in Liverpool*

*37. Liverpool Temperance Workers*

*38. Temperance Parade, Liverpool, July 1837*

is most optimistic. Success is measured mainly in terms of reductions in death rate. He believes that money spent on sanitation was well spent, there had been no very recent cholera outbreaks. He lists the great numbers of deaths due to infectious diseases in the population of 454,000 which included hooping (sic) cough 474, diarrhoea 649, scarlatina 400, tuberculosis 1600, and many many others. Six people died of gout, which would not be an acceptable cause of death today.

Violent deaths numbered 568 of these 384 were male, 184 female. Included in the total are 261 children. There were various causes for these deaths; wounds injuries etc 226, burns 28, drowning 66, murder 18, suffocation 94, excessive drinking 35. One wonders how sober many of the others were at the time of their death. Duncan discusses this point suggesting drink was indeed involved in many other cases e.g. of the 94 suffocated, 82 were infants, several mothers of these were intoxicated at the time. There were 23 suicides. Duncan then devotes a paragraph to intemperance, he records that 67 died of this condition, ages ranged from 10 to 70 and only two were "gentlemen". (Excessive drinking is not the same as intemperance, though the difference is not discussed).

Duncan notes the high mortality rates in Exchange and Vauxhall districts of Liverpool and compares these to the low rates in Rodney Street and Abercrombie. He believes the difference isn't just in sanitary conditions. Also important is the "proportion of Irish of the lowest class........the most filthy in their habits ...... so long as such an essential difference exists in the character and habits of the population of the two districts, no sanitary arrangements, however beneficial they may be, can ever reduce the mortality of the less healthy to that of the more healthy district".

To further his argument, he discusses how a comparatively Irish-free, working-class district of Liverpool can achieve as low a mortality rate as Ely (a town held up as an example to Liverpool). In his continuing discussion Duncan advocates sanitation and wants money spent on it, but uses the Irish as a scapegoat for poor results in specific areas. Irish, in a single word, seems to blanket many causes of social deprivation. In reading Duncan's criticism, one must remember that he was amongst the most enlightened and fair-minded commentators of the time. As Margaret

Simey writes "Dr. Duncan was one of the first to state publicly his opinion that the wretchedness of the Poor was the inevitable consequence of their circumstances and not necessarily their own fault…..".

In his 1860 report Duncan reports that suicides have increased from 23 to 37 but deaths due to intemperance have come down from 67 to 43, half of these due to Delirium Tremens. The 1861 report gives similar numbers but as Duncan points out, the Liverpool rate per head of population, is double that of London and 73% more than the eight principal towns of Scotland.

These figures may be supplemented by reference to the table "Indictable offences in Liverpool 1858" in Baines' *Liverpool in 1859*; shooting stabbing etc 200 cases, highway robbery 38, counterfeit coin 94, keeping disorderly houses 21, etc etc. The long list concludes with the offence of "Neglecting the family", there was just one case. Baines continues "Of the persons apprehended by the police 5486 belonged to Liverpool, 4861 to other parts of England, 8799 to Ireland, 1011 to Scotland, 791 to Wales, 142 to the Isle of Man and 899 to foreign countries. These figures reflected the mixed nature of Liverpool's wayward classes. It is also interesting to read the nationality of the police force; 581 English, 234 Irish, 94 Scottish and 61 Welsh. Seemingly none from the Isle of Man and no foreigners. Michael James Whitty, a Wexford man, was "not only Liverpool's first Chief Constable, but also the founder of the Police Force and Fire Brigade in Liverpool" in 1836 (M. Kelly 2003).

Frank Neal in his *Criminal Profile of the Liverpool Irish* gives a detailed and careful analysis of figures and definitions. While he agrees that in the legal system Catholics were disproportionately represented, crude figures are quite misleading. For instance 9,310 Catholics were committed to prison in 1876, but this represented only 710 individuals, recommittal was common. Offences were nearly always drink related, e.g. drunkenness, public order offences, assaults etc. Premeditated crime was unusual. He makes the point that comparisons of drunken behaviour between Liverpool and other cities is difficult. One reason is that in Liverpool drunken people in police cells were always brought before the magistrates. This was not the case in other northern towns, so direct comparisons are meaningless. He discusses the perceived causes of such behaviour. Some newspapers think it was purely due to religion (Catholicism) others saw it as purely racial (Celts).

W. Nott-Bower (1926) gives the Head Constable's view of drink and prostitution in late nineteenth century Liverpool. He feels that he had been berated by both sides, "The Trade" and the temperance movement, the latter he believed was "hostile" to his efforts. He opposes the 1875 changes when public houses were no longer inspected by the ordinary police but had special "inspectors" appointed to this role. These inspectors were underpaid and overworked, though their introduction was supported by the temperance movement. He gives a robust defence of his force against temperance critics who saw the police as being soft on licensees. He felt that public houses owned by the Brewers and run by salaried managers were best, there was no direct pressure to sell yet more alcohol but there was a desire for the business is to be run without complaint. Again the temperance party disagreed with this view.

**Dr. E.W. Hope**

In the 1906 report by Dr. Hope, it is recorded "A poster in the following terms was authorised by the City Council to be drawn up and posted on various advertising stations in the town".

*City of Liverpool*

*Abuse of alcohol*
*And its consequences*

*The City Council desires most urgently to call the attention of the citizens to the following facts: --*

*By order of His Majesty the King, a Report of a Special Committee was presented to both Houses of Parliament upon questions of health.*

*The enquiries of this Committee had proved that the abuse of alcohol is a most deadly agent. It lessens the strength and impairs the power for work of any kind. Everyone knows that all persons training for football or other athletics avoid alcohol.*

*Rum or other spirits in the early morning are most injurious.*

*Beer, wine or spirits should never be given to children or to infants.*

*The habit of drinking to excess leads to the ruin of the families, disgust for work, poverty, misery, theft, and crime.*

*Thousands of instances of cruelty to children occur annually in this City from the neglect and brutality of parents, often reduced to poverty through wasting their money on drink. These children in fact would be without clothes and without food, were it not for the action of charitable people*

*Alcohol is not in any sense a food, nor does it nourish the body in any way.*

There does not seem to be any evaluation of this attempt to reduce alcohol consumption and improve living standards. A more detailed poster was issued in Hull in the same year, discussed by Rutherford in *The Drink Problem*, a most wide ranging book edited by Kelynack (1906).

The annual reports published by successive Medical Officers of Health for Liverpool give figures for deaths due to intemperance. These numbers may indicate trends from year to year and are of some interest in relation to each other. They have no convincing value in absolute terms. Indeed it is recorded "Number of deaths does not indicate the extent of mischief caused by excessive drinking" (1909 report). The figures come from Coroners' Juries which have determined the cause of death to be due to excess drinking. Surprisingly those who died of "alcoholism" or D.T.s are not included in these numbers. Also excluded are numbers for fatal injuries, suicides, or even murders, occurring in people who were drunk. Many of the deaths occurred in the Workhouse or Hospital. Roughly speaking, males are 60%, females 40 % of the totals.

**Dr. W. S. Trench**

The 1863 figures are given by Dr. Trench. He sees fit to devote four pages of his report to a discussion on drunkenness. Trench's opening sentence has the problem in a nutshell. "Intemperance among the poor is at once a cause and a result of destitution", note he writes of the poor and immediately recognises the circular argument of cause and effect. However he then goes on to have a long discussion on industrial and monetary structures and the effect of these on drinking patterns - a little confusing.

**Dr. Francis Vacher**

Dr. Vacher was Medical Officer of Health in Birkenhead between 1873 and 1891 when he moved to act in a similar role for the county of Cheshire. He was a Scottish graduate in medicine and a man of wide interests. Apart from publishing extensively in his chosen profession (usually on Public Health or Temperance matters) he also wrote short stories, a book on engraving and was a Freeman of the city of London and past master of one of the old City Companies, all described in the *History of Birkenhead Literary and Scientific Society*. He chose startling titles for some of his papers, for instance "The Dead Body as a Source of Infection" and "Seduction in Edinburgh", he had qualified there in 1867.

He attended the 1884 National Temperance Congress in Liverpool speaking during the discussion on temperance in relation to young people. He had practical experience, in his professional life, of 10 year olds with drink problems. Today we read of huge increases in alcohol consumption by 11 to 15 year-olds (Front page, *Daily Telegraph* 27th Aug. 2005). He spoke of the need to influence such behaviour at the earliest possible opportunity. He also informed the Congress that he represented the newest of all the Temperance Organisations, "The Society for the Study and Cure of Inebriety". This had been founded some months earlier. The society aimed to gain a more exact knowledge of dipsomania than at present existed. It was hoped to achieve these ends by the study of the disease itself using a strictly scientific method. Hitherto, Dr. Vacher said, it had been usual to regard the person with the condition as of necessity a rascal, but that did not follow. The society which he announced came to produce a journal in which much research was published. This journal, under successive titles, is still publishing papers today. His appeal for open mindedness and scientific evaluation of the drink problem, was a breath of fresh air in an assembly often prone to personal prejudice and unsubstantiated claims.

Speaking at the 1895 Chester Congress Dr.Vacher drew together his ideas on alcohol abuse and insanitary living conditions. He attacked great medical men of the past who had believed alcohol could fortify the body against an unwholesome environment. He felt that people living in vile conditions became oblivious to problems because of drink. He concluded that if people avoided alcohol there would be a reduction in sickness rates and death rates for diseases such as stroke, bronchitis, liver disease etc.

**Dr. John Hay**

Dr. Hay was a medical officer in the Stanley Hospital, Bootle when he wrote a paper concerning his treatment of patients with pneumonia who had been admitted to the Mill Road infirmary between 1899 and 1901. His paper was published in the influential *Lancet* (11th of June 1904). The main thrust of his paper was to argue against the use of brandy in treating pneumonia. Such treatment was then the norm. Indeed he referred to a recent case when "an action for damages was taken out against a physician on the death of his patient because the patient had not received alcohol". He compared this with similar litigation in previous years when blood letting had not been used. Doctors were supposed to follow routine and give alcohol in the former case and let blood in the latter.

He argues strongly against medicinal alcohol while admitting that his personal conviction may be considered "heterodox and unorthodox" by his colleagues. He gives detailed figures for the survival rates of his 150 cases of pneumonia comparing those who are treated with alcohol with those who are not. The figures show those without alcohol fare far better in terms of survival, though survival rates are poor in comparison to today's outcomes, there were no antibiotics then. Dr. Hay is quite happy to use opium and hypodermic morphine for very disturbed patients.

He might consider alcohol but only in the later stages of rehabilitation, not during treatment for the acute condition. He has a fairly modern approach to compiling the two groups, (with and without alcohol). It is nearly a random controlled trial, where characteristics in both groups are very similar and treatment given, in this case alcohol, is not determined by the person in charge of the experiment. It is relevant that both groups similarly abused alcohol before admission. The results are " startlingly" in favour of no alcohol in treating acute pneumonia.

Dr. Hay was a pioneer in another aspect of medicine. When examining a case of pneumonia, he insisted on having the patient's chest fully uncovered. It was then generally feared that to so uncover could lead to the patient "catching cold" and worsening! Dr. Hay's views must have been well-received since he later became Professor of Medicine in Liverpool University and Deputy Lieutenant of the County Palatine of Lancashire before retiring to Bowness on Windermere. His son too became a Professor in the Medical Faculty of the University (John Shepherd 1972).

Dr. Nathan Raw, medical superintendent at Mill Road Infirmary in 1909, reviewed 3934 admissions suffering from mental illness. Of these, 1003 suffered from Alcoholism or Delirium Tremens (Charles Vaillant 1963).

**Dr. W. C. Sullivan**

Dr. Sullivan was deputy medical officer in Walton prison in 1899. He published his views on alcoholism, as seen from his prison service perspective, in 1906. He described the use of opium and spirits as stimulants, given to and used by, an "overworked and brutally used" workforce. Alcohol was seen both as a stimulant and as a sedative. Apart from ale, it was not easy to find fluids to satisfy thirst during hard physical work. Pure drinking water was not readily available and cholera epidemics were frequent. It was not in the interests of local publicans and others for there to be drinking fountains etc, though these were sometimes erected by philanthropic charities An interesting exception to this generalisation was in the case of Dandy Pat Byrne. He was a popular Irish local politician and the owner of several licensed houses. When he died, as a sign of appreciation, a fountain was erected outside his pub the "Morning Star" (M. Kelly).

The number of arrests for drunkenness, Sullivan believes, are a poor measure of the true problems caused by drink. Rather he feels that these numbers reflect the "Zeal of the police force and the amount of prison accommodation" available. In his professional position he should know.

He writes in detail on the consumption of drink by dock labourers, from their first awakening in the morning to the end of the working day. This averages 6 pints a day and excludes subsequent social drinking. He terms this drinking "industrial drinking". He goes on to describe how drink is provided for the dockers whilst at work. He claims that some shipping firms take direct control of organising the supply of liquor on their jetties. At the most basic level the daily cost of drink is booked and then deducted from wages. Sometimes, he says, the foreman guarantees the men's credit for drinking at a particular pub and this is then deducted on payday at that pub. The foreman gets 2/6d in the £1 from the publican (12.5%). Some pubs have their own tokens given to the foreman of the "tied factory". This is an interesting use of the word "tied". Usually the term is applied to the public house when it is tied to a particular brewery, i.e. has to sell only their beer. Here the factory or gang of dockers is tied to that pub. The foreman would then give out the tokens as an advance in wages to be used in that particular pub. Walton and Wilcox (1991) discuss Charles Mackay's view that it was the absence of lights and fires on ships in Liverpool's docks (because of danger of fire) that "drove sailors to beer houses in search of warmth and comfort".

Neil Todd describes in detail the various pub and cafe tokens available in Liverpool in the years 1853-1895. Similar tokens had existed since the 17th century. They were widely used in all manner of inns and taverns. Sometimes tokens would buy both entrance to a Musical Hall and also a certain number of drinks whilst there. F. W. Hackwood (1985) discusses these uses and describes various tokens, mainly those used in London and Birmingham. Today a similar system operates in some sports clubs, a plastic card serving as a "tavern check". Purchases are deducted, from previously invested money, on presentation of the card.

Dr. Sullivan has pleasure in describing an alternative method of providing credit for would-be drinkers. The treasurer of a total abstinence society lent out money so increasing the society's capital and a particularly beautiful temperance banner was purchased.

**Dr. James Shaw**

Dr. Sullivan described the adverse medical effects of drink which included "severe nervous disorders before the age of 40 "and touched on alcoholic dementia. Dr. Shaw was medical superintendent of Haydock Lodge. In 1891 he read a paper at the Liverpool Medical Institution. The title of his address was "Dementia: alcoholic, organic, and senile". It is to be noted that he puts alcoholic before organic or senile which may reflect his experience. One test he uses the differentiate tremor in these conditions is to give the patient alcohol. If the tremor subsides it is alcoholic dementia. He discusses force-feeding, "the patient may be fed for a considerable time by means of an india rubber tube passed along the floor of the nasal cavity and having a glass funnel ......". He continues, "occasionally patients will take food having been fed once in this way". The rest of his paper concerns neurological findings in alcoholism. He spends a little time discussing alcoholic amnesia (alcoholic blackouts).

**Dr. C. A. McBride (and ether addiction)**

The need to evaluate Fr. Matthew's work and pledge taking in general was acknowledged by Dr. McBride (1910). He quotes from the Journal of the American Society for the Study and Cure of Inebriety. "Ireland has in the 19th century presented to the world two interesting and remarkable series of inebrio-psychological phenomena. In 1838 a simple minded Roman Catholic priest Father Mathew adopted and began to advocate the practice of abstaining from all intoxicating drinks. (As a result) the duties of the military and police in Ireland were almost entirely confined to keeping the ground clear for the operation of Father Mathew".

McBride goes on to discuss outcomes resulting from abstention from alcohol. They include what we might today call drug substitution and solvent abuse. This was the second of the so-called inebrio-psychological phenomena mentioned above. McBride writes that "between 1842 and 1845 a local medical practitioner, in response to a request from a few newly pledged abstaining converts for something the taking of which would not violate their vow, gave them a dram of ether in water". The desire for more frequent doses grew upon these ether drinkers and the practice spread around other areas of Northern Ireland. In one town there was one shop for the sale of ether per 23 of the population.

A further reason for the popularity of ether was that the area had been a centre for the illicit distillation of whiskey. When this activity was suppressed, the whiskey drinkers turned to ether. Further cases were reported from Dublin, Glasgow, Lincolnshire and London. He believed that in Ireland ether tipplers were mainly the working class, whereas his cases in England were people of education and refinement. Ether inebriety occurred at all ages, including children. He reports that in Ireland, small shopkeepers treat children who have been sent to purchase of article, with a small dose of ether. Schoolmasters have detected ether on the breath of young children on arrival at school. Solvent sniffing by children has a long history!

McBride discusses the huge amounts taken, up to a pint a day. The preferred method he believes is inhalation in England, drinking the practice in Ireland. He continues by giving detailed accounts of administration and methods of distribution. Ether was mainly imported from England, large dealers then supplying small shopkeepers who in turn sold two spoonfuls at a time. Ether was available at fairs and other gatherings. He describes the effects of use on the human body, the desired and the pathological. He discusses preventative measures concerning the sale of ether. He quotes Norman Kerr, who is rather kinder to Father Mathew "the good and single hearted Theobald Mathew administered the pledge to 6 million Irishmen but a drink was introduced into the locality which it was asserted was harmless, not whiskey. Ether inebriates are to be seen today".

An account of ether's use in a more traditional and therapeutic setting, is given by M. W. Royden. He writes that in December 1846 news reached Liverpool about the successful administration of ether during an operation in Boston in the United States. Within days local surgeons were using the new technique and the next year a paper was given on its use at the Liverpool Medical Institution. The title of the paper was "On the Moral propriety of administering ether in other than extraordinary cases". Reservations about ether were particularly relevant to obstetrics. Beside the moral aspect there was a fear that insanity might be induced by ether.

**Opposition to Medical Opinion**

The arrestingly titled *Dialogues on Doctors and Drinking* (J. Whyte 1897), is not about doctors' personal drinking habits, rather it is a dialogue between two Scotsmen who together denounce the case for moderate drinking which had been made by "noted medical men". In this book the two suggest that Liverpool is the prime example of a city engaged in excessive drinking. They doubt if "20% of labouring classes are leading lives of restraint and decency". The usual details are recounted of the great proportion of income spent on drink. More interesting however is the subsequent widening of the debate. Does Liverpool really deserve her "bad eminence of being the most drunken town in England"? It is conceded that Liverpool's problems are known because "more attention has been given to the question of drunkenness and its causes in Liverpool than in most other towns". The discussants agree that any large town in England or Scotland could have a similar problem, if looked for, even in "our own pious, educated, sensible Scotch Glasgow"! Detailed accounts of the effects of drunkenness in Glasgow follow. They conclude that Birmingham and Belfast are even worse than Glasgow. Perhaps they have rehabilitated Liverpool, if only in as much as other big British towns are just as bad! M. S. Thompson (1988) provides a scholarly essay on these problems in nineteenth-century Edinburgh.

The *Liverpool Social Reformer*, a temperance periodical, between October 1871 and June 1873 describes various confrontations between Boards of Guardians and local doctors. A Dr. Costine attended the Toxteth Board and, though he himself had been teetotal for 40 years, he maintained that the use of spirits saved and prolonged lives, when he prescribed them. Another Board told their doctor that if alcohol were a medicine then he, not the Board, should pay for it. Upon this decision the doctor stopped ordering alcohol.

# National Temperance Congress Liverpool

In June 1884 a National Temperance Congress was held in Liverpool. By August the proceedings were published in a hardback which included all the papers given together with the subsequent discussions, the transactions of large public meetings and the sermons preached in local churches. A "lofty tone" was maintained from start to finish and every facet of temperance was examined! The Bishop of Exeter and Cardinal Manning filled Hengler's circus to overflowing (capacity 3000 - 4000). Local papers are said to have given daily and favourable comment on proceedings and "telegraphic summaries" appeared in the national press. Liverpool's success led to further congresses e.g. in London 1886, Birmingham 1889 and Chester, 1895. The close similarity of these congresses, e.g. Chester 1895, to conferences held in Liverpool in recent years, has been discussed by M. T. Malcolm 1991.

Papers presented to the Congress were grouped into different subjects e.g. "The Scientific Phases of Temperance". The measurements and descriptions used are far more colourful than in today's publications. Dr. Benjamin Ward Richardson, then the leading light of the movement, spoke in this section. He reported that a man who drank 4 ounces of alcohol per day had 12,960 extra heartbeats which he believed was equivalent to his lifting 15 tons, a foot off the ground. He implied that this was undesirable. He didn't consider the physical labouring and alcohol consumption of an average Liverpool docker.

A more realistic account comes from the casualty surgeon of Edinburgh Royal Infirmary. "Most" patients who attended were intoxicated and drink had been major cause of accidents. How little has changed.

**Rev. J. A. Macfadyen**

Rev. Macfadyen gave a detailed account of brothels and prostitutes in Manchester and Liverpool, Liverpool had double Manchester's provision! He considers the effect of drunkenness on gross national product, "Foreigners say that Providence has arranged that our race shall be handicapped by the love of drink in order that other races may have a chance against us". No reference is given for his contention. The national drink bill he believed was £220 millions. He calculated that three years of such spending "if deposited in the Bank of England and carried away in one-horse carts ...... required 2716 carts, each with 25 cwt of sovereigns ..... in a procession 12 miles long". Another way of considering Scotland's expenditure on drink was to consider what could have been purchased instead; One million yards of linen, calico, check, flannel, and corduroy; .... half a million pairs of socks, hats; .... four million loaves, pecks of oatmeal; thousands of sheep, cows etc etc. We are not today familiar with such comparisons, made in scientific papers, perhaps we should be.

**Cardinal Manning**

Cardinal Archbishop Manning presided over the section "Legislative Remedies for Intemperance". His opening remarks included "The legislature has been building up a great scaffolding around the drink trade .... become a partner in the whole business .... sanction to a vast amount of evil". Because of revenue gained the Government was " a sleeping partner in that trade". He believed everyone shared in the Government's guilt. Though the Cardinal had begun by saying " we are not come here to make speeches today we are come to confer" his, clearly political, remarks covered ten pages of text in the book. He held in his hand a list of bills presented to the House of Commons which had been rejected, bills intended to curb the sale of alcohol. Drink was everywhere, even the railway was becoming a "travelling tavern". At the end of October 2005 it was proposed to ban alcohol on trains, so as to curb bad behaviour by drunken youths. The alternative view was that such a blanket ban would preclude those dining from having a glass of wine, or those celebrating opening champagne. Are class issues still relevant?

The Cardinal continued his political tirade at the Hengler's Circus public meeting. "We Christians .... are the only men on earth that are stained and shamed by the manufacture and consumption of intoxicating drink ... . The great Indian, Oriental, Chinese, and Mohammedan populations ... the four great worlds of man, by their law and their religion were bound not to take intoxicating drink..... wheresoever the Christian name had spread, intoxicating drink had followed." He then moved on to opium abuse. "In China persons were poisoned with opium, which was forced upon them year after year by diplomatic treaty, and by an imploring voice they had called upon the British Government to cease from poisoning their people. Three times they had taken up arms against us to preserve themselves from this pestilence. Again, in British Burma, where, before England entered, it was death to sell intoxicating agents such as opium, now the trade was more or less free. Opium had been forced upon the Burmese.....".

**Youth Work**

The next speaker gave a history of the Young Abstainers' Union, 1879 to 1884. There were 76 branches with nearly 8000 members. Class is again most important, "Numbers do not constitute standard of success we could double or treble numbers but it is a limited company". Limitation was applied in two ways, a special introduction was required and there was a statement regarding the "certain classes of society we desire to work among … the sons and daughters of the upper and middle-class … being careful not to tread on the ground already occupied by the Band of Hope workers". A list of rules followed for "drawing-room meetings, summer garden parties" etc. There were existing branches in New Brighton, Waterloo, Liverpool East, Sefton and Princes Park.

A more realistic paper concerning work with the young then followed, "Juvenile Temperance Work in Liverpool" which gave an interesting history, from October 1830 onwards, of the various societies based in Liverpool. It was concluded that "There are, within 8 miles of Liverpool Town Hall, 211 Bands of Hope and Juvenile Societies with an enrolled membership of 51,000.

The Church of England Temperance Society was then particularly concerned about female intemperance, so a "servants' branch was formed". There were 85 such branches in existence. Evidence was presented as to the effectiveness of temperance on working habits, e.g. improved attendance at work after festive week-ends. There was even a branch specially for "girls at restaurants and railway refreshment bars" and there were plans for "girls who served in public houses". Passive smoking was not then an issue.

At the other end of the social scale Mrs Green of Liverpool Ladies' Temperance Association reported on 20 years of activity. These ladies met fortnightly and employed four missionaries, one was sent to the police courts devoting her time to women who in consequence of drink appeared before the magistrates. There were also visits to parents concerning prevention of cruelty to children. On the other hand, "Special work for women of the better classes was done in a quiet way ... ".

**Practical Alternatives**

The importance of having an alternative to drink, other than austere abstinence, was discussed during the session "Auxiliary Aids to Temperance". It was acknowledged that such alternatives would tempt men away from their proper place, in the home, when not at work. However, healthy alternatives were better than the ever present public house and its consequences. The president of the session acknowledged that "Liverpool was nearly foremost in cheap entertainment for the people on the Saturday evenings having established cheap concerts at the hall in Lord Nelson Street more than 40 years ago". He went on to praise the Church of England Temperance Society which was working effectually in inducing farmers and others to pay the whole of the workmen's wages in money, and not any part in beer, cyder or other intoxicating drinks.

The secretary of the Liverpool British Workman's Public House Company (Limited) reminded the Congress that the Company's formation had followed the visit of Moody & Sankey to Liverpool in 1875. It had then been noted that 20,000 men, employed on the docks, had no place of shelter except the public house. The company had started with a working capital of £20,000 in £1 shares. It worked on commercial lines, prices were fixed as low as possible to ensure the patronage of the working classes. Initially there were no hot dinners, merely comfortable accommodation for those who brought their own food, hot drinks were provided. The first house had accommodation for 1000 customers. Attention was then turned to railway stations, markets and other busy places and gratifying results were obtained such that there were 60 branches in operation. During the previous year over £85,000 had been gathered in halfpence and pennies, showing the sort of trade undertaken. It was said that 25,000 services were made daily in the various branches.

The hours of business were from 5 a.m. until 11 p.m. "The early morning business is of great value; the trading done from 5 to 7 a.m. is often worth the rest of the day's taking and as the public houses cannot commence business until 6 a.m. they get a full hour's start". It was believed that the 5 a.m. start prevented a breakfast of "rum and milk". Five a.m. might seem an early start, but it was not unusual, medical pupils (students) were expected to attend lectures which began at 5 a.m. (Ormerod *History of Liverpool Medical School*).

The whole staff employed by the company, 400 persons, were all pledged abstainers. There was a notice over the bar saying that The Pledge could be signed there at any time. The account continued, describing how Sir W.B. Forwood had suggested that the attention of the Company be turned in the direction of the Exchange where large numbers of drinking bars existed. A better style of cafe was opened there which proved most successful.

An alternative source of nutrition in Liverpool, for many years, had been soup kitchens. Grisewood, secretary to the Liverpool Central Relief and Charity Organisation Society, frequently mentioned in his annual reports, in the 1870s, that the Cocoa Rooms were taking trade from these kitchens, which the Society supported. The police had been given 1500 soup tickets to give to "cases of urgent distress". However by 1878 the Society faced reality and gave "a number of Cocoa Room penny tokens" (to be distributed to cases of extreme want).

An update on the Company was given to the National Temperance Congress at Chester in 1895 by Rev. Charles Garrett. There were then 65 houses and the capital was £50,000. A dividend of 10% was usually paid. Pressure to open on Sundays had been experienced, but the directors refused to open on the Sabbath, though their arch-enemies, the pubs, were open. The success of houses in the Exchange area had led to further outlets in up-market shopping streets where large and high-class custom was obtained.

R. G. Milne (1982) has reviewed the company's annual reports etc. He discusses the compatibility of evangelical Christianity with a 15-17%

profit margin, (10% paid to investors). He also gives an interesting account of the use of tokens and vouchers, (given as part payment of wages or as charity) to be used in these temperance facilities. The company was at its height in 1907 when it had 87 outlets, 14 of the Cocoa Rooms offering lodging accommodation. In 1922 it became the well-known City Caterers and in 1978 it was taken over by Ladbrokes, not a teetotal organisation.

**Women and Drink**

Mrs Pratt of Liverpool spoke on this subject under the title "Inebriate Homes For Women". She believed that women, being more impulsive than men, were probably more difficult to reclaim but that the reclamation was not impossible. A Mrs Theobald working in Leicester had had some success treating upper and middle-class women. More appropriate for Liverpool was the account given of the Vergmont Sanatorium, Stanley, Liverpool which had been opened for 3 years. The Liverpool Ladies' Temperance Association had found it most useful even though " many of the women are handed over from the police courts in a destitute condition". Chloral and opium patients had also been successfully treated. Most of the 94 cases from the working classes seem to have done well.

**Church Services**

The book concludes with a list of 112 churches and chapels on Merseyside where sermons on temperance were preached. This shows something of the religious activity in the Liverpool region at the time as well as the wide range of denominations. Another list comprises the 87 Sunday Schools and Children's Services where temperance was discussed. At St Peter's Catholic Church in Seal Street the priest said that he had been prevented from speaking fully on temperance because he had to read a letter from His Holiness concerning Freemasonry.

# End-piece

Valid conclusions about Victorian temperance workers cannot be drawn from the above accounts as individuals have been selected largely on account of their colourful use of language or their flamboyant behaviour. They are not representative of the main body of temperance advocates.

Sometimes in the 19th century, abstinence was enforced by employers on their work force, or by builders on house buyers. However the temperance crusaders had to use persuasion in an attempt to change the habits of an independently-minded population, whose consolation during a hard life was often supplied only by the public house. Today people are even more free, even more demanding of their rights and choice of behaviour. They have more disposable income to spend on drink. Consumption in Britain is escalating, though not so in other European countries.

Problems due to drink are increasing in terms of damage to an individual's health or damage to society in general. In spite of this, proposals to increase availability of alcohol, so-called 24-hour drinking, come into force in November 2005. Clearly "The Trade" would not increase hours, unless there was more profit to be made, i.e more alcohol sold. The goverment which made the law also benfits financially in the short-term; costs will be elsewhere, e.g on the roads or in hospital departments.

In Victorian Britain the views of local people, (local option), were usually in favour of restriction of alcohol availability, yet the licensing benches and "The Trade" ensured there was no restriction. Little has changed. *The Times* newspaper September 6th 2005 reports that while the great majority of people, (62%), do not support longer licensing hours, the Government and local councils continue to support even greater access to drink.

# Further Reading, Victorian and Modern Texts

Books on the history of the Temperance Movement fall mainly into two groups, the early personal accounts and modern, more critical, reviews. For full details see “References”.

***The History of the Temperance Movement in Liverpool and District from its Introduction in 1829 down to the year 1887***, was written by Peter Turner Winskill and contains 126 pages of dense text. Even that, according to the author, was a summary of “a mass of useless verbiage and waste rubbish”, he was referring to his sources, which had included a trawl through local newspapers. He claims to write free from any bias of “creed, sect, party or nationality”. Winskill published widely on the subject of temperance history but in the Liverpool volume he is co-author with Joseph Thomas of 200 Scotland Road. The latter had personal involvement in Liverpool’s temperance activity having lectured on the subject and collected relevant papers and periodicals over his lifetime. The book was reprinted from a series of articles previously published in the *Liverpool Mercury*. The authors claimed that since no one had contradicted their accounts, the resulting book must be an accurate history, but later authors have questioned some of its contents.

An extended summary of his book is now given because no copy of the book seems to be available on Merseyside. There are four copies in the extensive Livesey collection in Preston.

Liverpool’s Temperance Society is said to date from July 22nd 1830, Glasgow Bradford and Warrington societies had been formed earlier that year. However Winskill claims there is evidence to suggest that the Liverpool Society was under active consideration *before* the formation of the other societies. In December 1829 three American Sea Captains reported favourably on Temperance Societies in the U. S. A. to a meeting in the Bethel Union, Liverpool. At a second meeting there, in March 1830, a provisional committee was formed leading to the July meeting when a full committee was formed. Winskill records all their names.

In 1831 the Rev Nathaniel Hewitt, representing the American Temperance Society, visited Liverpool with a view to the formation of a British version. He was able to obtain the patronage of the Bishop of Chester. Society members were to "pledge ourselves to relinquish spirituous liquors except for medicinal purposes". They recognised the difference between temperance and abstinence by adding that though wine and malt liquors were not forbidden it was considered that excessive use must exclude one from membership. This difference was to become a major and divisive issue.

Medical support was quick in coming. Winskill reproduces a declaration signed by many of Liverpool's leading physicians and surgeons in November 1831. "We…are of opinion that one of the principal causes of the pauperism, crime, and disease which now exists among the working classes of society in this country is intemperance". Doctors in many other towns had already signed similar declarations.

Winskill continues with a most favourable review of John Finch's work, a Mr Wetherspoon working with him in urging abstinence on dock labourers. Winskill makes a particular point of detailing the meeting between John Finch and Mr Swindlehurst in Preston. He reproduces a long, detailed, verbatim account of what is supposed to have been said at their first meeting. Winskill concludes "Preston was indebted to Liverpool receiving its first inspiration from Mr Finch". It is usually believed that Preston preceded Liverpool in temperance organisation.

Winskill reproduces one of Finch's many letters to the local press concerning the dreadful plight of the drunken working-class as seen during visits to their homes. Later letters concerned similar visits in Preston. The experience gained during these visits enabled their authors to write with first-hand knowledge and sympathy. These letters may be seen as forerunners to Hugh Shimmin's later writings.

The next few chapters concern the development of total abstinence as opposed to temperance. Various towns vie with each other for the honour of having originated the ideal of total abstinence. Winskill believes Skibbereen in Co. Cork had the first recorded total abstinence society, in 1817. More and more of the northern towns came to advocate total abstinence, though the British and Foreign Temperance Society in London, as late as 1848, refused to acknowledge or adopt the "fanatical doctrine of the Lancashire enthusiasts". Winskill reports that some members of the Society were "brewers and others making and selling intoxicating liquors", hence their support of temperance rather than total abstinence. Very many meetings, in rooms and halls all over Liverpool are described in detail. There appeared to be a fragmentation of meetings and societies until, in 1836, it was proposed to amalgamate together as "The Liverpool Total Abstinence Society", (medicinal and "religious" alcohol was still allowed). Discussion of politics and religion were to be strictly avoided, a pity that this aim was not always followed in the future. In spite of this attempted rationalisation many and varied societies continued to be formed. Possibly this lack of cohesion prevented the planned Temperance Hall becoming a reality in 1836.

So powerful was the influence of the "temperance party" in Liverpool that in 1836 liquor dealers organised themselves into a special society the "Anti-Temperance Society" and commenced a publication entitled the *Anti Teetotaler*. It did not last long.

Winskill's next chapters concern John Finch's missionary work in England, Ireland, Scotland and Wales; he started total abstinence societies all over the United Kingdom. Finch made a speech on the folly of sectarianism, which was becoming rife in Temperance Societies.

In 1837 the Catholic clergy of Liverpool were asked to sanction the formation of a Catholic abstinence society. In their reply the clergy expressed great support for the plan but added "To a desire intimated in the said memorial that the clergy themselves subscribe the pledge on the secret understanding of their not being bound strictly to observe it, they reply.......". There then follow reasons why the clergy have no need to sign the pledge! The society was most successful, by the following year, 1838, there were 1792 members.

On the 16th of July 1838 there was a grand parade and Winskill lists all the local bands that played. Three thousand people walked in a procession for six hours through the main streets of Liverpool. On one corner they played the *Dead March* in memory of a drunken man who had been killed there by his drunken friend the previous week.

Opposition to temperance meetings is described. For example numbers of men, drunk from a neighbouring brewery, disrupted a meeting; worse was a shower of stones! More subtle were lectures given by clergymen who didn't believe in total abstinence. One of these was the Rev. Hugh M'Neile (sic). The *Liverpool Mercury* published a letter from a Dublin gentlemen to M'Neile. In it, he proposes a public debate with M'Neile because the latter had said that total abstinence was calculated to lead men to destruction quoting scripture to support his contention. Sadly no response to this challenge is mentioned.

The work of James Ackland is described. He was editor of the *Liverpool Politician* and the *Liverpool Teetotal Times*, he also advocated the idea of a ship canal from Liverpool to Manchester. Winskill continues with a detailed account of religion and, unfortunately, sectarianism as they affected the Temperance and Abstinence movements in Liverpool. He felt that in Liverpool certain persons "were more anxious for the promulgation of their own narrow creeds than temperance principles".

Winskill again writes in praise of John Finch who was being increasingly rejected by religious colleagues. Finch was much influenced by the socialist, Robert Owen. He describes Finch's later life, up to his death and burial in the Ancient Chapel of Toxteth in 1857 aged 73. An even more detailed description of Finch and his work is given in Winskill's Addenda.

In February 1839, the "Howard Total Abstinence Society" was formed. The aim was to introduce the principles of total abstinence to the "middle and upper classes of society". It was composed of clergy, medical men and respectable inhabitants.

Attempts were made to have sober crews on ships. Seventy per cent of accidents and losses at sea were caused by drunkenness. Insurance companies gave a 5% premium if there were no spirits on board. Captains might even refuse to take sailors who were not total abstainers.

Winskill, having admitted that he identified with Methodism from boyhood, felt he should record that the Wesleyan Methodist chapel in Pitt Street Liverpool rented its basement to a wine and spirit dealer. Even then Liverpudlians where able to write witty graffiti. A placard was posted on one of the Chapel doors:

*There's a spirit above and a spirit below,*
*The spirit of love and the spirit of woe;*
*The spirit above is the spirit divine,*
*But the spirit below is the spirit of wine.*

Further quotations from ministers opposed to absolute abstinence follow. Rev Mr Whitty, a Protestant clergyman, opposed Father Mathew's administering the temperance pledge on the Rock of Cashel, saying that such activities were the work of the devil. Winskill gives an account of Father Mathew in Liverpool in 1843. At an open-air public meeting beside St.Anthony's, Scotland Road, Matthew, Rev Amos Phillips of Boston and Rev Mr Blanchard of Cincinnati addressed the crowd. A year later a similar meeting was held, again with an American speaker. By 1844 temperance lectures included diagrams and coloured drawings exhibiting healthy human organs and, for comparison, those diseased by alcohol. Father Mathew's 1849 visit to Liverpool involved a close association with William Rathbone. The latter even "nobly and generously removed some of the difficulties by which (Mathew) was at that time surrounded". One imagines these to be largely financial. Mathew gave the pledge to a number of people at Greenbank, Mr Rathbone's residence.

Chapter 17 is largely devoted to discussing further American connections, in particular the Sons of Temperance Friendly Society. American members of the society came across to help establish branches in Liverpool. In 1849 two branches were formed and by 1851 there were 10 divisions in Liverpool, two Unions for the Daughters of Temperance and five sections of the Juvenile Order. From Liverpool the society spread to all parts of Britain.

Between1850 and 1855 a variety of new temperance organisations were established, of varying duration and of different religious denominations.

William Rathbone continued to urge that temperance be seen as non-sectarian. The Temperance League was trying to influence the town council and magistrates to reduce the number of licences. As Winskill put it "moral suasion must be supplemented by legislative enactment rigorously, persistently, and impartially enforced". The need for legistative action is supported by his next statement "society after society was organised and renewed efforts made, but still the masses were steeped in drunkenness".

In October 1854 Father Mathew arrived again. However he was too ill to receive a purse containing a hundred guineas at a public meeting so he received it at Greenbank. The Earl of Sefton contributed £20 towards his convalescence in Madeira.

Liverpool magistrates in 1855/6 would not allow public processions through the streets, so grand galas etc were held in Claughton Park, Birkenhead. Detailed descriptions are given of these festivities. Winskill quotes the editor of the *Liverpool Chronicle* concerning the magistrates and the licensing system, "The whole system is rotten to the core. Licensed houses combine the features of the brothel the grog shop and the gin palace, places of the demoniacal atrocity".

In October 1860 the celebrated American phrenologist Mr L. M. Fowler lectured on temperance at the Concert Hall in Lord Nelson Street. Winskill discusses the 1863 canvas of householders in Liverpool concerning Sunday closing. He gives detailed tables and figures concerning this comprehensive survey of opinion. It is interesting to read that labourers, mariners and shopkeepers were largely in favour of Sunday closing, professional gentleman and merchants were less so.

Between 1856 and 1865 there was some decline in temperance activity, "listlessness and indifference". Why should this be? Public demonstrations and festivals had been prohibited by the magistrates. Further the magistrates "wilfully and flagrantly pandered to the wishes of the wealthy brewers". Thirdly many of the older workers had been lost. In September 1865 a large public meeting protested against the "so called free trade licensing system recently introduced by the magistrates of Liverpool". In 1867 Mr S. R. Graves MP introduced a " Liverpool Licensing" bill aimed at restricting licences in a variety of ways. It was unsuccessful. Rev John Jones published his famous "*The Slain in Liverpool by Drink*". A further household survey in 1869 showed massive support for a reduction in licences, the magistrates' response was to publish a drunkard list containing the names and addresses of those convicted of drunkenness - published in the *Mercury* of Tuesday. It was ineffective.

In 1872 there was further activity as regards Catholic societies for abstinence, Archbishop Manning and Father Nugent were involved. The Father Mathew Society ensued. The League of the Cross was also founded by Father Nugent. Less easy to understand are the various American based Templar branches whose names were regularly changed.

At a more practical level Mr R M'Dougal opened a dining-room, run on temperance principles, in Renshaw Street which was a great success. Further branches were opened but the businesses were later sold. The British Workman Public House movement originated in Leeds in 1867 but Winskill believes that Liverpool pioneered these houses operating on sound commercial principles. Further impetus to these arrangements was given by Moody & Sankey's mission. Winskill describes this in detail. (See chapter on "National Temperance Congress Liverpool").

In 1876 the temperance movement decided to offer temperance candidates for seats on the Toxteth Board of Guardians, to oppose the sitting five publicans. The temperance candidates opposed the provision of intoxicating drinks in the workhouses and the appointment of doctors who prescribed brandy and beer! In 1877 six temperance candidates were elected. One of their first actions was to discontinue the system whereby the chief officers and nurses had two pints of beer per day, inferior officers, one. These workers accepted money instead.

Prohibition was introduced to various areas of Liverpool by means of clauses inserted into leases concerning residential development. Upper Warwick Street and Parliament Fields had in their leases a requirement for absolute prohibition. Winskill describes other large tracts of Liverpool which were free of all aspects of the liquor trade.

During a week's conference in 1879 Liverpool played host to visitors from all over the world; Florida, India, Massachusetts, New South Wales, New Zealand, Norway, South Australia, South Carolina, Virginia, Ontario, Nova Scotia, etc. A hundred years later similar International Conferences are still held in the city.

Another well-known crusader was Mr Nathaniel Smyth whose *Drink Map of Liverpool*, published in 1883, is discussed. Its wide circulation, showing excessive numbers of drink outlets in the "squalid part of the city" but few in the areas where the magistrates lived, prepared the way for "local option" developments. In 1885 the publication *Drink Plague in Liverpool* further emphasised the evils of drink, tabulating the various problems brought before magistrates and coroners and their close association with public houses. A detailed description of the National Temperance Congress Liverpool 1884 is given, (discussed already).

In his final chapter Winskill concludes that much successful work had been achieved, often against a variety of vested interests including organised religion, medical opinion, commercial interests, political parties, and social habits.

At the end of his book there are various Addenda. Many of these concern John Finch, e.g. his definition of a drunkard, "a human being that gets drunk and if it gets drunk frequently it is an habitual drunkard. Drunkards are of three kinds: poor drunkards, female drunkards, and gentlemen drunkards". This, apparently simplistic definition, is then enlarged upon during several pages of text which give an overview of Finch's perception of the whole problem.

Winskill reprints from the *Preston Temperance Advocate* Finch's account of his tour of Ireland where a Catholic priest advocated a glass of whiskey and the use of ale and wine in moderation. In Cork he spoke at Mr W. Martin's Teetotal Society in 1836 no mention being made of Father Mathew though the names of Rev. Dunscomb and a Catholic priest called Rev. Mr Scanlon are given as being active in the movement.

Finch appears a little grandiose when he proclaims himself "King of the Teetotallers of Ireland, Scotland, Cumberland and Liverpool". His reasons for this claim are then spelt out; he formed 100 societies of which they were 100,000 members. The remainder of his claims are written somewhat tongue in cheek, they make interesting reading.

In 1838 there were two Female Temperance Societies which held weekly meetings. "No males except the Chairman and Secretary were allowed to be present. Ten females were on the platform and perhaps 600 females in the audience". (For a more detailed account of contemporary views of the effect of alcohol on women and children see Mary Scharlieb 1907).

A full account of temperance entertainments in Bootle is given. Mr and Mrs Poulsom opened a Cocoa Room in Derby Road in 1877. Concerts were given twice a week and the success was such that by 1866 the Town Hall was being used to entertain up to 1500 persons.

***The Temperance Movement and its Workers; a Record of Social, Moral, Religious, and Political Progress*** Blackie and Son London 1891-2. This is Winskill's major historical account. Four volumes, each of nearly 300 pages. There are many fine portrait engravings and many references to Liverpool. Available locally in Liverpool.

***The History of Liquor Licensing in England.*** Sidney and Beatrice Webb in their classic history discuss Liverpool's contribution to licensing law. They describe reduction in licences by the Liverpool's magistrates in 1821, followed by the famous increases of the 1860s, made in the name of free trade. Their appendix is interesting. Lest it be thought that the temperance movement arose de novo in the 1830s, they describe the "Societies for the Reformation of Manners" which had as their aim "the encouragement of piety and virtue, and for the preventing and punishing of vice, profaneness, and immorality". These associations flourished between 1690-1710, 1786-95 and again from 1802. Drunkenness was the common denominator. But as the Webbs write "this repressive activity was wholly directed against the drunkenness and immorality of the humbler classes, not against the licentiousness of the rich". They discuss the view that the Justices were just as "infected".

## Modern Texts

***Drink and the Victorians - the temperance question in England 1815 - 1872,*** Brian Harrison (1971), provides a detailed discussion of the motives behind those advocating temperance. He describes class issues but does not see the temperance movement simply as attempting to impose middle-class manners on the working-class. A wide variety of vested interests are keen to keep drinking habits unchanged. He groups the early campaigners into evangelicals, industrialists, doctors and coffee traders. He thinks all had mixed motives and allegiances. He discusses the economics of drinking and of abstinence and shows how the temperance movement interrelated with many other political developments. American, Scottish and Irish influences are also included. He has a most helpful table, showing the dates of operation of various temperance organisations. A further table shows how temperance activists were also associated with a variety of other philanthropic activities. He discusses the role of the (nanny) state as opposed to individual choice. There are many references to Liverpool's involvement. This is one of the main works on the subject.

***Crusade Against Drink in Victorian England*** by Lilian L. Shiman (1988) provides the standard history of the temperance movement. She describes the shift from moderation through total abstinence to prohibition and the interactions between the churches, (established and nonconformist) and the links to political parties. Drink became a problem to be addressed when it interfered with production, after the industrial revolution. In the 1830s the middle-class and ministers of religion led but by the 1840s the working class were in charge. She traces the development of legislative methods and the involvement of temperance workers in local politics. She too discusses the balance between self responsibility and the role of the state in anti-social behaviour. Again there is a vast reference section.

***Low Life and Moral Improvement in mid-Victorian England: Liverpool through the Journalism of Hugh Shimmin*** by Walton and Wilcox (1991) contains a series of contemporary articles by the journalist and later owner of the *Porcupine*, Hugh Shimmin. The articles have particular relevance to drink and entertainment as experienced at that time. The editors' introduction gives a detailed analysis of Shimmin and the views he formed. They believe his outlook must have been influenced by his upbringing. When he and his mother arrived in Liverpool, to join his father, they found him "stupefied by drink in a pub". His mother, a Primitive Methodist, was later active in the temperance movement. Walton and Wilcox praise the descriptive accounts given by Shimmin but repeatedly point out that statistics are not his forte, also that he tends to ignore other influences relevant to the behaviour of Liverpool's lower classes. They write "drink is at the core of Shimmin's analysis of social pathology" adding that he believed the role of local government was to suppress public and commercial temptation to drunkenness. Though they question how first-hand some of his evidence really was, they conclude that he was "one of the most stimulating of the qualitative social observers of mid-Victorian England".

***Father Matthew and the Irish temperance movement 1838-1849*** by Colm Kerrigan (1992) provides an impressively researched account of the man, his life's work and the problems he faced. Whilst there are many books on Father Matthew this is perhaps the standard work of reference and makes most interesting reading.

***The Albert Dock and Liverpool's Historic Waterfront*** by W. R. Cocksfoot (1994) describes the widespread drunkenness among nearly all who worked on the docks. The corporation constables drank on duty and fought with the drunken watchmen. Pubs catered for different types of drinkers, local Liverpool roughs or smart American coloured seamen.

***Liverpool a People's History*** by P. Aughton (1990), a beautifully illustrated book, details Liverpool's Marine Humane Society, which was mainly involved in the rescuing of near-drowned people using two "newly invented pumps for drawing poisonous liquors or ardent spirits from the stomach, when taken to such excess as to produce suspended animation" (It is to be remembered that the father in *Her Benny* drowned while drunk). This immediate treatment in the community may have been better than admission to hospital, even if such were possible. Nurses were often drunk and police had to patrol the wards to try and reduce the smuggling in of further supplies of drink. To improve Liverpool hospital conditions Rathbone imported Florence Nightingale who successfully improved matters. Her work was continued by the famous Agnes Jones 1865. Aughton pictures statues of Cannon Major Lester and Fr. Nugent facing each other in St John's Gardens.

***Building Jerusalem, the rise and fall of the Victorian City,*** by T. Hunt (2004), discusses the Irish working-class in big Victorian cities, especially Liverpool and Manchester. He quotes at length from Engles "the race that lives in these ruinous cottages……wet cellars, in measureless filth and stench……this race must really have reached the lowest stage of humanity". Engles saw their homes as pig sties and Irish women and children as swine. He believed Irishmen didn't want decent housing or clothing just drink. They are "little above the savage, contempt for all human enjoyments …..all favour drunkenness". The main part of the book is a fascinating account of the development of the Victorian city.

***Democracy and Sectarianism a Political and Social History of Liverpool 1868-1939,*** by P. J. Waller (1981), includes an account of the Liverpool temperance movement's support for "education in domestic science and sanitation, free libraries, sports clubs, saving banks and friendly societies". Such facilities would lead to less need for public houses. The essential guide to Liverpool's social history.

***Politics and Elections in Nineteenth-Century Liverpool,*** by Neil Collins (1994) describes the interactions between political parties, religion and the temperance movement in the city. There appears to be tolerance towards buying drinks for voters (treating), not so for bribery. By 1868 all the Liberal candidates gave a temperance pledge. However Collins feels "the electoral appeal of the temperance movement alone does not seem to have been very great".

***Licensed to Sell, the History and Heritage of the Public House***, by Geoff Brandwood, Andrew Davison, and Michael Slaughter, published by English Heritage (2004). A beautifully illustrated book on public houses. In describing the development of the pub, the authors give an account of legislative restrictions on alcohol sale. They also include a discussion on the temperance movement together with temperance hotels etc. There are many photographs of public houses in Liverpool and Birkenhead.

***Alcohol and Temperance in Modern History an International Encyclopaedia,*** Blocker et al. (eds.) (2003).This two volume 769 page work shows the interest developing, certainly in America, in the history of temperance.

# Acknowledgements

My grateful thanks to previous writers whose work I have freely used even to the point of plagiarism. The omissions and misinterpretations are mine. Sincere thanks also to my teachers H. McC, F.B and especially J. S. M., initials so as not to embarrass them by my mistakes. Thank you to the staff of Liverpool, Birkenhead and University of Central Lancashire, Preston libraries and to Liverpool Medical Institution for storing, cataloguing and retrieving obscure works.

Illustration sources. Thanks to Livesey collection, Univeristy of Central Lancashire, Preston (and to A.T-B.) for no's 1-7, 18, 21, 22, 24 & 38, and to Liverpool Record Office for numbers 8, 10-12, 15-17, 19, 20, 31, 32 & 36.

# References


Armstrong, R. C. "The Deadly Shame of Liverpool, an Appeal to the Municipal Voters". Pamphlet 1890.

Aked, Rev. C. F. "England free and Sober". (Temperance League Pamphlet). Lee and Nightingale, North John St., Liverpool 1897.

Aspinall, H. K. "Birkenhead and its Surroundings". Liverpool Booksellers Co., Liverpool 1903.

Aughton, P. "Liverpool, a People's History". Carnegie, Preston 1990.

Baines, T. "Liverpool in 1859; The Port and Town of Liverpool, and the Harbour, Docks, and Commerce of the Mersey". Longman and Co., London 1859.

Barr, A. "Drink; an Informal Social History". Bantam Press, London 1995.

Bass, Ratcliff and Gretton Ltd. "Excursion to Liverpool and New Brighton", republished by The Bass Museum, Burton-upon-Trent, 1977.

Belchem, J. "Merseypride: Essays in Liverpool Exceptionalism". Liverpool University Press, Liverpool 2000.

Bennett, Canon, "Father Nugent of Liverpool". Liverpool Catholic Children's Protection Society 1949. (see also Runaghan, P. "Father Nugent's Liverpool 1849-1905". Countyvise, Birkenhead 2003.)

Best, G. "Mid-Victorian Britain 1831 -- 1875". Granada Publishing, Panther Books, St. Albans Herts.1973.

Birkenhead Literary and Scientific Society 1857 to 1907, History of. Privately published by the Society, Birkenhead 1907.

Blocker, J.S., Fahey, D.M., and Tyrrell, I.R. (eds.), Alcohol and Temperance in Modern History: an International Encyclopaedia. Santa Barbara, CA 93117, Dec. 2003.

Boyle, T. "Black Swine in the Sewers of Hampstead". Hodder and Stoughton, London 1990.

Brandwood, G., Davison A. and Slaughter, M. "Licensed to Sell, the History and Heritage of the Public House". English Heritage, London 2004.

Brendon, P. "Thomas Cook, 150 years of Popular Tourism". Secker and Warburg, London 1991.

Burke, T. "Catholic History of Liverpool ". Tinling and Co., Liverpool 1910.

Campbell, J. "F. E Smith, First Earl of Birkenhead". Jonathan Cape, London 1983. (Pimlico ed. 1991).

Cavanagh, T. "Public Sculpture of Liverpool". Liverpool University Press, Liverpool 1997.

Cockcroft, W.R. "The Albert Dock and Liverpool's Historic Waterfront". Print Origination, Formby 1994.

Cologan, W. H. and Cruise, F. R. "The Catholic Temperance Reader". Catholic Truth Society, London 1900.

Collins, N. "Politics and Elections in Nineteenth-Century Liverpool". Scolar Press, Aldershot 1994.

Duncan, W.H. "Report on the Health of Liverpool During the Year 1859", (and subsequent years). George McCorquodale and Co., Liverpool 1860.

Forwood, W. B. "Recollections of a Busy Life". Henry Young and Sons, Liverpool 1910.

Graham, J. " The Secret History of Alcoholism". Element, Shaftesbury Dorset 1996.

Grisewood, W. "Annual Reports of Liverpool Central Relief and Charity Organisation Committee". Haswell, C., Liverpool 1887,1888.

Hackwood, F. W. "Inns, Ales and Drinking Customs of Old England". Studio Editions, London 1985.

Hawthorne, N. "Our Old Home". William Paterson, Edinburgh 1884.

Hart-Davis, A. "What the Victorians Did For Us". Headline Book Publishing, London 2001.

Harrison, B. "Drink and the Victorians. The Temperance Question in England 1815-1872". Faber and Faber, London 1971.

Hocking, S. K. "Her Benny". Various editions over many years.

Hubbard, E. "The Albert Dock". Illustrated Liverpool News, August 1971, 17 number133, (no page).

Hughes, Q. "Liverpool". Studio Vista, London 1969.

Hume, Rev. A. "Condition of Liverpool, Religious and Social: including notices of the state of education, morals, pauperism and crime". Brakell, Cook St., Liverpool 1858.

Hunt, T. "Building Jerusalem; the Rise and Fall of the Victorian City". Weidenfeld and Nicolson, London 2004.

Jones, Rev. J. "The Slain in Liverpool during 1866 by Drink; also Social, Medical and Criminal statistics of drunkenness". (Reprinted from the Liverpool Mercury). Barker and Co, Liverpool (n.d.).

Jones, J. R. "The Welsh Builder on Merseyside Annals and Lives". J. R. Jones, Cintra, Menlove Ave., Liverpool 1946.

Kaighin, J.R. "Bygone Birkenhead; Sketches Round and About the Sixties". Willmer Bros., Birkenhead 1925.

Kelly, M. "Liverpool; the Irish Connection". Print Origination, Formby 2003.

Kellynack, T.N. (ed.) "The drink Problem in its Medico-sociological Aspects". Methuen, London 1907.

Kerrigan, C. "Father Mathew and the Irish Temperance Movement 1838 -1849". Cork University Press, Cork 1992.

Kirton, J. "The Young Abstainers Reciter; Dialogues, Recitations, and Readings Suitable for Anniversary, Social, and Other Meetings". Ward Lock & Co., London (n.d.).

Lundie, R. H. "The Dark Side of Liverpool". Pamphlet, Liverpool 1880.

Lundie, R.H. "Alexander Balfour A Memoir". Oliphant Anderson Ferrier, Edinburgh 1895.

McBride, C. A. "The Modern Treatment of Alcoholism and Drug Narcotism". Rebman, London 1910.

Macalister, C. J. "Liverpool Royal Southern Hospital". W.B. Jones & Co., Liverpool 1936.

Maguire, J. F ."Father Mathew a Biography". Eason and Son, Dublin 1882 (first edition 1863).

Mays, J. O'D. "Mr. Hawthorne Goes to England: The Adventures of a Reluctant Consul". Ringwood, 1983.

Meacham, S. "Regaining Paradise: Englishness and the Early Garden City Movement". Yale University Press, New Haven 1999.

Miller, A. "Poverty Deserved? Relieving the Poor in Victorian Liverpool" Liver Press, Birkenhead 1988.

Milne, R. G. "The History of the British Workman Public House Company Limited, The Liverpool Cocoa Rooms". Typescript in Liverpool Central Library, 1982.

Morris, M. and Ashton, J. "The Pool of Life, a Public Health Walk in Liverpool". Dept. Public Health, Liverpool 2002.

Muir, R. "A History of Liverpool". Williams and Norgate, London1907.

Munro, A. and Sim, D. "The Merseyside Scots". Liver Press, Birkenhead 2001.

"National Temperance Congress Liverpool 1884". National Temperance Publication Depot, London 1884.

"National Temperance Congress Chester 1895". National Temperance League Publication Depot, London 1895.

Neal, F. "A Criminal Profile of the Liverpool Irish" Trans. Historic Society of Lancs. and Cheshire. 140, 161-199, 1991.

Nottingham, L. "From Merchant to Banker 1742 to 1992". Rathbone Brothers, London 1992.

Nott-Bower, W. "Fifty-two-Years a Policeman". Edward Arnold, London 1926.

O'Connor, F. "A Pub on Every Corner" vols.1 2 3 4. Bluecoat Press, Liverpool 1995-97-98 and 2001.

O'Mara, P. "The Autobiography of a Liverpool Irish Slummy". Martin Hopkinson, London 1934.

Ormerod, H.A. "The Early History of the Liverpool Medical School 1834 to 1877". C. Tinling and Co. Ltd., Liverpool (n. d.).

Picton, J. A "Memorials of Liverpool". Gilbert Walmsley, Liverpool 1903.

Porter, R. "The Drinking Man's Disease; The Pre-History of Alcoholism in Georgian Britain". British Journal of Addiction 80, pp385-396, 1985.

Pratt, E. A. "The Licensed Trade". John Murray, London 1907. (see also " Licensing and Temperance in Sweden Norway and Denmark ". 1907.)

"Price's of Bromborough 1854 to 1954". Balding and Mansell, for Price's of Bromborough 1954.

Rathbone, E. F. "William Rathbone A. Memoir". Macmillan and Co., London 1905.

Richardson, A.J. "The Major Public Buildings of England and Wales. No.1, St. Georges Hall". West Derby Publishing, Liverpool (n.d.).

Richardson, B. W. (ed.) in "The National Temperance Congress Chester 1895". National Temperance League Publication Depot, London 1895.

Richardson, B. W. "Public School Temperance". The Grip Printing and Publishing Company, Toronto 1887.(For use in Ontario).

Rose, R. B. "John Finch,1784 - 1857; A Liverpool Disciple of Robert Owen". Transactions of the Historic Society of Lancashire and Cheshire vol. 109 pp 159-184, 1958.

Royden, M. W. in "Wives and Whores in Victorian Liverpool". Liverpool Medical History Society, Liverpool 1999.

Sargant, W "Battle for the Mind ". Pan Books, London 1957. (see also "The Mind Possessed". William Heinemann, London 1973).

Saundby, R. "Old Age its Care and Treatment in Health and Disease". Arnold, London 1914.

Scharlieb, Mary. "Alcoholism in Relation to Women and Children", in "The Drink Problem". Kellynack, T. N. (ed.) Methuen, London 1907.

Sharples, J. "Liverpool ". Yale University Press, 2004.

Shaw, J. " Dementia, Alcoholic, Organic and Senile". Proceedings of Liverpool Medical Institution, 23 pp299-321, July 1892.

Shepherd, J.A. "A History of the Medical Institution". Bemrose Press, Chester 1979.

Shiman, L.L. "Crusade Against Drink in Victorian England". MacMillan Press, London 1988.

Shimmin, H. "Low Life and Moral Improvement in mid-Victorian England: Liverpool Through the Journalism of Hugh Shimmin". Walton, J.K. and Wilcox, A. (eds.) Leicester University Press, Leicester 1991.

Simey, M.B. "Charitable Effort in Liverpool in the Nineteenth Century". At the University Press, Liverpool 1951.

Smith, S. "My Life-Work". Hodder and Stoughton, London 1903.

Strachey, L. "Eminent Victorians". Various editions, 1918.

Sullivan, W. C. "Alcoholism a Chapter in Social Pathology". James Nisbet, London 1906.

Thackeray, W. M. "The Irish Sketch Book". Smith, Elder and Co., London 1887. (1st edition 1843).

Trench W. S. "Medical Officer of Health Reports". Greenwood , 32 Castle St. and Hewson & Proctor, Leather Lane, 1866-1877.

Thompson, M. S. "The Wages of Sin; the Problem of Alcoholism and General Paralysis in Nineteenth-Century Edinburgh", in "The Anatomy of Madness". Bynum, W. F., Porter, R., Shepherd, M. (eds.). Routledge, London 1988.

Todd, N. B. " Tavern Checks from Liverpool and Vicinity". Liverpool Museum, Liverpool 1987.

Vaillant, C. M. "An Historical Sketch of the Emergence of Liverpool Psychiatry". Journal Liverpool Psychiatric Club, pp1-16. Oct. 1963.

Waller, P.J. "Democracy and Sectarianism a Political and Social History of Liverpool 1868-1939". Liverpool University Press, Liverpool 1981.

Walton J.K., and Wilcox A. (eds.) "Low Life and Moral Improvement in mid-Victorian England: Liverpool Through the Journalism of Hugh Shimmin". Leicester University Press, Leicester 1991.

Webb, S. and B. "The History of Liquor Licensing in England Principally From 1700 to 1830". Longmans Green and Co., London 1903.

Whyte, J. "Dialogues on Doctors and Drinking". John Hayward, Manchester 1897.

Wilson, A. N. "The Victorians". Hutchinson, London 2002.

Winskill, P.T. "The Temperance Movement and its Workers" 4 volumes, Blackie and Son, London 1891.

Winskill, P.T. and Thomas, J. "History of the Temperance Movement in Liverpool and District from its Introduction in 1829 down to the year 1887". Joseph Thomas, 200 Scotland Road, Liverpool 1887.

Yates . "Yates Brothers Wine Lodges Ltd.1884-1984". Yates, 1984.

## References for Illustrations
## (for sources, see acknowledgements)

**Front cover.**

The Workshops of Baccus, or the Drinking Customs of Society.
(from a large poster).

**Back Cover.**

Description of Alcohol.
(John B. Gough's pamphlet).

**1 The Drunkard's Children.**

(George Cruikshank, Nat. Temp. Public Depot, 1881).

**2 The Drunkard's Children.**

(George Cruikshank, Nat. Temp. Public Depot. 1881).

**3 Intemperance, step the fifth.**

(Brit. Foreign Temp. Intelligencer, 9 Nov I839).

**4 Take a Public House.**

(Ipswich Temp. tract No.43).

**5 Intemperance, step the second.**

(Brit. Foreign Temp. Intelligencer. 12 Oct. 1830).

**6 Death Unmasked.**

(Supplement to Temp. Advocate, July 1836).

**7 Temperance and Intemperance.**

(Brit. Foreign Temp. Intelligencer, 28 Mar. 1840)

**8 Rev. John Jones's pamphlet.**

**9 Rev. R. H. Lundie.**

**10 Rev. R. A. Armstrong's pamphlet.**

**11 Armstrong's second pamphlet.**

**12 Cannon Abraham Hume.**

**13 John Finch.**
(The Temperance Movement, Winskill, i, p.134)

**14 Thomas Swindlehurst, "King of the Reformed Drunkards".**
(The Temperance Movement, Winskill, ii, p.I46).

**15 Hope Hall**

**16 Advert. For Non- Alcoholic Sacramental Wine.**
(L'pool Soc. Reformer, 1872 p. 81).

**17 Liverpool Medical Institution & Hope Hall.**

**18 Map of Liverpool's retail alcohol outlets.**
(Nathaniel Smyth)

**19 Liverpool Social Reformer, the Organ of the Temperance Movement.**

**20 Notice of Public Meeting.**
( L'pool Social Reformer, 1 Dec.1872 p. 45).

**21 Thomastown House, Father Mathew's birthplace.**
(A Brief Memoir of John Giles, Joseph Glass, Judd and Co. Fleet St., London n.d.).

**22 Rev. Theobald Mathew.**
(Postcard issued by Lemonade manufacturers, Nassau Place, Dublin).

**23 William Rathbone.**
(William Rathhone a Memoir, Eleanor Rathbone, Macmillan and Co. London 1905).

**24 Map of USA (at the time of Father Mathew's visit).**
(The Struggle, No.36, 1842, J. Livsey, Preston, sold by Britton, 34 Paradise St., Liverpool).

**25 H. K. Aspinall.**
(Birkenhead and Surrounding, Liverpool Booksellers Co. 1903).

**26 Clark Aspinall.**
( The Temperance Movement, Winskill, iv, p. 210).

**27 W. B. Forewood.**
(Recollections of a Busy Life, Henry Young, Liverpool 1910).

**28 Samuel Smith.**
(My Lifework, Hodder and Stoughton, London 1903).

**29 Thomas Cook.**
(The Temperance Movement, Winskill, i, p. 248).

**30 Temperance Gathering at Overton Hill, near Chester.**
(The Illustrated London News, 19 June 1858, p. 601 ).

**31 Dr. E. W. Hope.**

**32 Dr. W. S. Trench.**

**33 Dr. F. Vacher.**
(History of the Birkenhead Literary and Scientific Society, published by the society, printed by E.Griffith and Son Ltd, Hamilton Street ).

**34 Dr. John Hay.**
(Liverpool & Birkenhead in the 20th Century, W.T. Pike & Co. Brighton, 1911).

**35 Cardinal Manning.**
(The Temperance Movement, Winskill, ii, p. 188).

**36 British Workmans Coffee Tavern in Liverpool.**
(The Graphic, 12 Jan. 1878).

**37 Temperance Workers in Liverpool and District.**
( Temperance Movement, Winskill, ii, p. 210).

**38 Temperance Parade in Liverpool, Lord Street, 20 July 1837.**
(Preston Temperance Advocate Vol. 10 Oct.1837).